I0813413

Family Recipes for Year-Round Festivities

ROSSELLA RAGO

Cooking with Nonna

CONTENTS

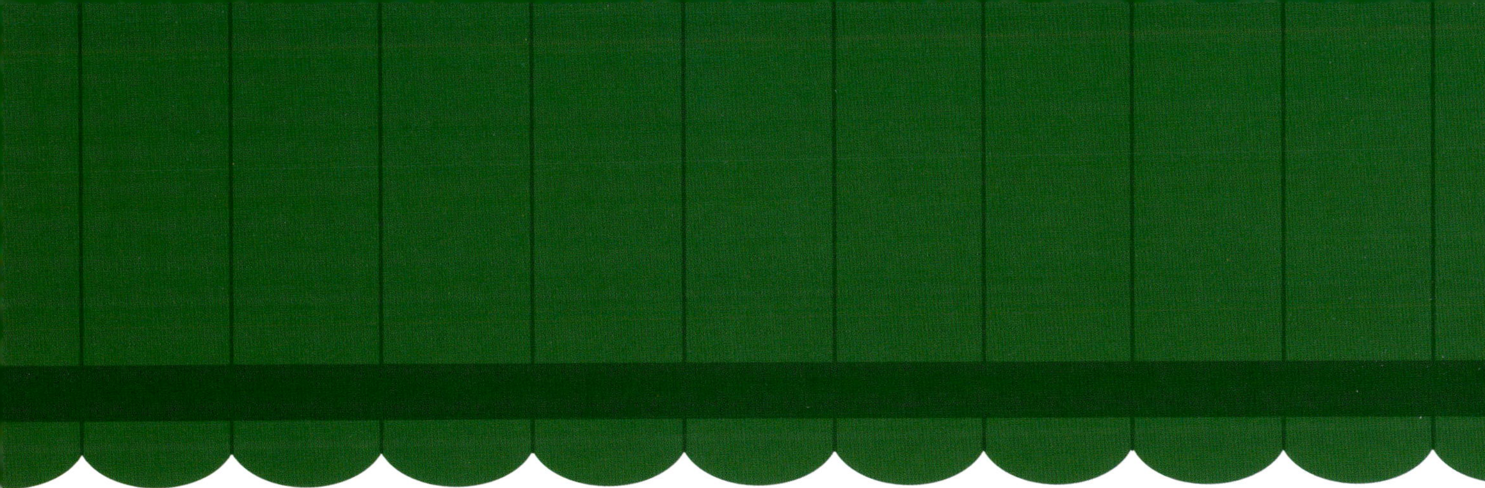

INTRODUCTION

For Italians, every holiday is a chance to come together as a family and enjoy one another. We eat, we drink, and we reminisce, but most importantly, we love!

The Italian Celebration Cookbook is a collection of holiday recipes, stories, and memories from some of the incredible nonne who serve as the cornerstone in every Italian-American family. Whether you're baking cookies in the kitchen with your nonna as she tells you a sweet story of holidays gone by or frantically yelling at someone because they forgot to buy lemons at the supermarket, the magic of the holidays will always bring out the passionate side of Italians.

Italy is a country rich in tradition, especially when it comes to the holidays, and I wanted this book to be a go-to guide for putting together a holiday meal, Italian-style. The chapters are organized by holiday instead of course, because every holiday has its own unique flow of ingredients and traditions behind the recipes. I had the opportunity to meet a number of incredible ladies who shared their own families' histories and heritages while I wrote this book. Many of the dishes on these pages have evolved with time and have been adapted to suit a particular family's palate or circumstances.

Feel free to be adventurous with any of the recipes, because by doing so, you'll begin to forge holiday recipe traditions of your own. I cannot tell you how many people write to me during the holiday season feeling regret that they can't seem to get something to taste exactly like their nonna's rendition. My response is usually the same for everyone: "That's totally fine, because I'm sure your nonna used to say the same thing about matching her own nonna's skills, and one day your grandchildren will say the same thing about you!"

The recipes in this book will take you through a year of Italian holidays, through the lenses of the incredible nonne who make our holidays so special in the first place. They celebrate the meaningful moments in life, whether it be with a fabulous cookie for Christmas Day or a humble bread made as an offering to a saint. While there are over one hundred recipes in this book, I wish I could have included hundreds more to adequately represent the vast beauty of the Italian holiday landscape. Each nonna was so excited to share her recipes and stories with me, and ultimately with all of you. I hope you adopt at least one of these recipes as your own so that it lives on with your families and creates as many special memories for you as these recipes have for me. In the words of my Nonna Romana: "*Figlia bella di nonna, durante le feste si creano i ricordi piú belli.* (Throughout the holidays, the most beautiful memories are made.)"

Nonna Giulia Rotondi's

GIARDINIERA

PICKLED MIXED VEGETABLES

Prep time: 16 hours, plus 2 to 3 weeks preserving

Yield: 4 quart (960 ml) jars

Giardiniera is a mix of vegetables preserved in a vinegar brine that Italians refer to as *sottaceto* (under vinegar). Nonna Giulia always has her pantry stocked with a few jars for when company drops by unexpectedly (which is often). They make a wonderfully effortless antipasto when paired with olives and cheeses, and she usually sends her guests home with a jar or two, like an Italian-style party favor or *bomboniera*.

3 pounds (1.4 kg) red bell peppers, stemmed and seeded, cut into ¾-inch (2 cm) dice

3 pounds (1.4 kg) green bell peppers, stemmed and seeded, cut into ¾-inch (2 cm) dice

3 pounds (1.4 kg) yellow bell peppers, stemmed and seeded, cut into ¾-inch (2 cm) dice

3 pounds (1.4 kg) eggplant, peeled and cut into ½-inch (13 mm) dice

2 pounds (910 g) celery, cut into ¼-inch (6 mm) dice

3 tablespoons salt

Juice of 5 large lemons

14 cups (112 ounces/3.3 L) white vinegar

35 cloves garlic, sliced

1 cup (140 g) capers, drained

1 cup (96 g) coarsely chopped fresh mint

1 tablespoon red pepper flakes

4 cups (960 ml) extra-virgin olive oil, plus more as needed

1. In a large bowl, add the bell peppers, eggplant, celery, salt, and lemon juice; toss well with a spoon. Cover the bowl with plastic wrap and let it rest for 4 hours at room temperature.
2. In a large colander, drain the vegetables, using a large dish to press out the liquid. Drain for about 5 minutes.
3. To a large bowl, add the vegetables and the white vinegar. Let marinate for 3 hours at room temperature.
4. Drain the vegetables in the colander once again. Put a large plate over the vegetables and place weights equal to about 40 pounds (18 kg) on it. Leave the weights on the plate overnight.
5. Add the garlic, capers, mint, and red pepper flakes and mix well; distribute evenly between the jars. Fill each jar with 1 cup (240 ml) of the olive oil, adding more as needed to cover all the vegetables. Cover the jars and store for 2 to 3 weeks before serving.
6. Serve chilled or at room temperature. Refrigerate the jar after opening.

Nonna Lydia Palermo's

CREMA PASTICCERA

PASTRY CREAM

Prep time: 5 minutes
Cook time: 10 minutes
Yield: About 2 cups (480 ml)

Nonna Lydia makes the smoothest, most velvety pastry cream I have ever tasted. In Italy, this basic cream with light notes of citrus and vanilla is used to fill countless pastries and cakes. The secret is using cornstarch instead of flour, which can give the cream a bit of a chalky taste and is more likely to create lumps. For most desserts, you can easily make the cream the night before and store it in the refrigerator. Just let it come to room temperature before using it.

6 tablespoons granulated sugar
3 tablespoons cornstarch
1 cup (240 ml) whole milk
1 tablespoon heavy whipping cream
3 large egg yolks, beaten
1 teaspoon vanilla extract
Whole peel of 1 lemon

1. In a medium bowl, whisk together the granulated sugar and cornstarch. Set aside.
2. In another medium bowl, whisk together the milk, cream, beaten egg yolks, and vanilla extract until incorporated.
3. In a large saucepan over medium heat, warm the milk-egg mixture and the sugar-cornstarch mixture, stirring continuously with a wooden spoon. Add the lemon peel and continue stirring until the mixture thickens, 7 to 8 minutes. Remove from the heat. Remove and discard the lemon peel and continue to stir for another 30 seconds.
4. Press a sheet of plastic wrap onto the surface of the cream. Let cool to room temperature.

Nonna Lydia Says

If you made your cream the night before and you find that it has a few lumps, you can either push it through a fine-mesh strainer with a spoon or do a quick mix with an electric mixer.

Nonna Lydia Palermo's

CREMA DI RICOTTA

CANNOLI CREAM

Prep time: 10 minutes
Yield: About 4 cups (960 ml)

This classic Sicilian cannoli cream is a mixture of sheep's milk ricotta, confectioners' sugar, and maybe some semisweet chocolate chips, and is used in cannoli, among other things. Over the years, Nonna Lydia's family has tweaked the recipe to add a little more flavor with some notes of orange, vanilla, and cinnamon. This recipe also calls for *ricotta impastata*, which has been naturally drained of excess moisture to produce a smooth, velvety cream. If you can't find it, regular ricotta will do.

2 pounds (910 g) ricotta impastata
1½ cups (180 g) confectioners' sugar
1 packet (½ ounce/15 g) Italian vanilla powder or 1 teaspoon vanilla extract
½ teaspoon ground cinnamon
½ teaspoon orange extract
½ cup (90 g) mini semisweet chocolate chips (optional)

1. In a large bowl, combine the ricotta impastata, confectioners' sugar, vanilla, cinnamon, and orange extract. Mix well and then pass the mixture through a strainer to smooth out the texture.
2. Fold in the chocolate chips (if using).

Nonna Lydia Says

If you like the cream a little sweeter, add up to 2 more tablespoons of confectioners' sugar; don't use more than that because it will melt and make a runny cannoli cream.

Nonna Laura Fosco's

ESTRATTO DI LIMONI

SWEET LEMON ZEST

Prep time: 15 minutes
Yield: 1 jar (6 ounces, or 180 ml)

The first time I baked with Nonna Laura, she reluctantly allowed me to shop for the ingredients she needed. I purchased a little bottle of lemon extract as she asked, but upon arriving to her darling house in Astoria, Queens, she instructed me to return it and get my money back for two reasons: 1. "It's expensive!" and 2. "I make!" She pulled a jar out of the refrigerator with a small, faded label on it that said, "Nonna Laura's Sweet Lemon Zest." It was basically a mixture of freshly zested lemons, some lemon juice, and a bit of sugar. A nonna with her own product line? My heart melted! This little jar of heaven will save so much time zesting lemons during your holiday baking.

Freshly grated zest of about 24 medium to large organic lemons

Juice of 4 lemons

2 tablespoons sugar

Add the lemon zest, juice, and sugar to the jar, making sure the juice barely covers all the zest. Store in the refrigerator for up to 2 months.

Nonna Rosa Carmelo's

VIN COTTO

FIG OR WINE SYRUP

Prep time: 5 minutes
Cook time: 6 hours
Yield: About 10 cups (85 ounces, or 2.4 L)

Vin cotto (cooked wine) is a thick syrup made throughout southern Italy, usually out of wine, wine must, or even figs. The fig variety is technically called *cotto di fichi*, but in my family we always used the term vin cotto. It is primarily used in desserts, such as *cartellate* (page 161), and is regarded as something of a precious commodity in my family. In Italy, my Bisnonna Regina would always make gallons of vin cotto to be sold in her bottega for the holiday season. I still have such vivid memories of my Zia in Mola di Bari making vin cotto from the figs that bloomed in late August. This event usually heralded the end of summer vacation, and it was always my job to "smuggle" the vin cotto into the States. Today, my Zia Rosa is notorious for her "bootleg" vin cotto.

2 gallons (7.5 L) prune juice or wine must

1 In a large, wide, stockpot with a lid, bring the prune juice, covered, to a boil over medium-high heat. Once boiling, uncover, reduce the heat to low and simmer until the juice has reduced by two-thirds and thickens enough to coat the back of a spoon, about 6 hours. Let cool to room temperature. The syrup will further thicken as it cools.

2 Once cooled, pour the syrup through a fine-mesh strainer and funnel into a glass bottle. Store in a cool, dry place for up to 8 months.

NEW YEAR'S EVE AND DAY

VALENTINE'S DAY

Nonna Rosa Vella's

COTECHINO CON LENTICCHIE

COTECHINO SAUSAGE WITH LENTILS

Prep time: 5 minutes
Cook time: 45 minutes
Yield: 6 to 8 servings

Most Italians believe in the old superstition that eating lentils on New Year's Eve will bring wealth and good fortune for years to come, owing to their disk-like shape that resembles a coin. Nonna Rosa fiercely believes in this and never skips a year. "I no wanna take no chances, but I eat a lotta lentils and I'm still waiting for the money," she jokes as she unwraps a fresh *cotechino* sausage. Cotechino is a rich pork sausage that hails from the Emilia Romagna region. Most people buy a precooked cotechino that is vacuum-packed, but now, many butchers carry the fresh variety, which is superior in flavor and easy to prepare.

1¼ pounds (567 g) cotechino sausage, not precooked

3 tablespoons extra-virgin olive oil

4 cloves garlic, sliced

2 ribs celery, cut into ½-inch (13 mm) dice

1 medium carrot, cut into ½-inch (13 mm) dice

1 small red onion, cut into ¼-inch (6 mm) dice

3 or 4 leaves fresh sage

2 tablespoons chopped fresh parsley

16 ounces (455 g) dried lentils, rinsed and picked through

1½ teaspoons salt

Black pepper

1. Prick the cotechino all over with a fork, then place it in a small heavy-bottomed pot and cover it with water. Bring to a boil over high heat, then boil, uncovered, for 45 minutes.
2. Meanwhile, in another small pot with a lid, heat the olive oil over medium heat. Add the garlic and cook for 30 seconds. Add the celery, carrot, onion, sage, and parsley. Cook, stirring occasionally, for 1 to 2 minutes. Add the lentils and cook, stirring occasionally, for another 2 minutes. Add 5 cups (1.2 L) of water, the salt, and black pepper to taste. Cover and cook until the lentils are tender and most of the water has been absorbed, about 30 minutes.
3. Transfer the cotechino to a plate, remove its outer skin, and slice and serve over the lentils.

Nonna Romana Sciddurlo's

PANZEROTTI

MOZZARELLA AND TOMATO FRITTERS

Prep time: 1 hour 5 minutes
Cook time: 8 minutes
Yield: 6 servings

Every summer I look forward to eating this special street food, which is comparable to the Italian-American calzone. With every bite, gorgeous strings of fresh mozzarella ooze from the golden crust, which is light as a feather. Families from Puglia also make these for both New Year's and Christmas Eve.

DOUGH

2 tablespoons extra-virgin olive oil, plus more for greasing

1 packet (¼ ounce/7 g) active dry yeast

2 cups (240 g) all-purpose or 00 flour, plus more for dusting

1 teaspoon salt

FILLING

6 ounces (170 g) fresh mozzarella cheese, shredded

½ cup (50 g) grated Parmigiano-Reggiano cheese

½ cup (75 g) cherry tomatoes, cut into ¼-inch (6 mm) dice

1 tablespoon capers (optional)

Black pepper

Olive oil, for frying (or any frying oil you like)

1. **To make the dough:** In the bowl of a stand mixer fitted with the dough hook attachment, combine the olive oil, yeast, and ¾ cup (180 ml) of water. Let stand until the yeast is dissolved, 5 to 8 minutes.
2. In a medium bowl, whisk together the flour and salt. With the mixer running at low speed, slowly add the flour to the yeast mixture. Mix until a smooth, supple dough forms, 8 to 10 minutes.
3. Grease a bowl with olive oil. Shape the dough into a ball, place it in the bowl, and brush it with olive oil. Cover with plastic wrap and set aside until the dough has doubled in size, about 1 hour.
4. Transfer the dough to a floured work surface and knead for 2 to 3 minutes. Cut the dough into six 2-ounce (55 g) pieces. Roll each piece into a ¼-inch-thick (6 mm) round. (Don't worry if it isn't perfectly round; you will adjust the shape later with a ravioli cutter.) Reroll any scraps.
5. **To make the filling:** Add 2 tablespoons of mozzarella to the center of each piece of dough. Follow with 1 tablespoon of Parmigiano-Reggiano and 1 tablespoon of diced tomatoes. Add 4 or 5 capers (if using). Season with black pepper and fold the dough over to create a pocket.
6. Seal the edges around the filling by pressing with your fingers or the floured tines of a fork. With a ravioli cutter, trim the edges, leaving a border about ½ inch (12 mm) wide. Gather any scraps from the edges to make more panzerotti. Lay the panzerotti on a floured baking sheet and cover with a dish towel.
7. Heat 1 inch (2.5 cm) of oil in a small heavy-bottomed pot over medium-high heat. Working in batches, fry until golden brown, about 2 minutes per batch. (Make sure to fry the panzerotti as soon as you finish making them or else you risk the dough drying out and splitting open in the oil.)

Nonna Romana Sciddurlo's

PALLINE DI SAN MARZANO

NO-BAKE ALMOND SAN MARZANO BALLS

Prep time: 20 minutes
Yield: About 48 balls

This incredibly easy recipe was created by my Nonna Romana and perfected by my mother, Angela. Ground almonds are mixed in cocoa powder, sugar, and San Marzano, a liqueur from Puglia. We used to have to smuggle San Marzano into the United States ourselves, but now it's more readily available. It was my mother who had the brilliant idea to use hot cocoa mix or Nesquick to easily achieve that sweet chocolatey flavor. This is the perfect, slightly boozy dessert to make if you're entertaining on New Year's Eve and don't want to spend all night in the kitchen. Be careful though, they're stronger than you think!

- 16 ounces (455 g) whole blanched almonds
- 10 ounces (283 g) hot cocoa mix
- ¾ cup (180 ml) San Marzano liqueur or any amaro you prefer
- Granulated sugar, for rolling

1. In a food processor fitted with the blade attachment, process the almonds until finely ground (but not a flour-like consistency), about 2 minutes.
2. In a medium bowl, combine the processed almonds and the hot cocoa mix. Add the liqueur and mix well until a soft paste forms.
3. Place the sugar in a shallow dish. Roll the almond paste into balls about 1 inch (2.5 cm) in diameter. Roll the balls in the sugar and transfer to a clean plate.
4. Refrigerate for about 1 hour and serve cold.

Nonna Romana Says

If you can't find San Marzano liqueur, you can substitute any sweet liqueur you desire, such as amaretto, Baileys Irish Cream, or even Marsala wine.

Nonna Angelina Purpura's

SFINCIONE SICILIANO

SICILIAN PIZZA

Prep time: 1 hour

Cook time: 1 hour

Yield: 6 to 8 servings

DOUGH

2 packets (1/4 ounce/7 g each) active dry yeast

3 cups (720 ml) warm water

2 tablespoons extra-virgin olive oil, plus more for greasing

4 cups (668 g) semolina rimacinata

2 cups (240 g) all-purpose or 00 flour, plus more for dusting

1 tablespoon salt

SAUCE

2 tablespoons extra-virgin olive oil

1 medium onion, finely chopped

1 can (28 ounces/794 g) crushed tomatoes

1/2 teaspoon salt

1/2 teaspoon dried oregano

1/4 teaspoon black pepper

SFINCIONE

1/4 cup (27 g) plain bread crumbs

1 cup (100 g) large-grated plus 2 tablespoons grated Parmigiano-Reggiano, divided

1 teaspoon dried oregano

1/4 teaspoon black pepper

18 anchovy fillets packed in olive oil, drained and fillets halved

1/2 cup (120 ml) extra-virgin olive oil

Sfincione is a thick-crusted Sicilian pizza—a bit like *focaccia*. Nonna Angelina tops her golden semolina crust with savory anchovies, Pecorino Romano cheese, and a delicious sauce with lots of oregano. The bread crumb topping melts into the cheese and creates a soft, creamy texture like no other. It's usually prepared through Christmas and New Year's in the Palermo area, but Angelina makes two or three trays at a time for almost every holiday because it's that good!

1. **To make the dough:** In a small bowl, combine the yeast and the warm water and let dissolve for 5 minutes. Grease a baking sheet with olive oil.
2. In a large bowl, whisk together the semolina flour, all-purpose flour, and salt. Slowly pour the yeast mixture into the bowl and stir until a sticky dough forms.
3. Turn out the dough onto a floured work surface and knead until smooth, 7 to 10 minutes. Add the 2 tablespoons of olive oil to your hands and the dough, and knead until the oil has been somewhat incorporated, 2 to 3 minutes. Transfer the dough to the baking sheet and, using your hands, press it out from the center into an even layer. Cover the pan with a kitchen towel and let rest in a warm, dry place for 1 hour.
4. **Meanwhile, make the sauce:** In a large saucepan, heat the olive oil over medium heat. Add the onion and cook, stirring occasionally, until translucent, 5 to 7 minutes. Add the tomatoes, salt, oregano, and black pepper, and stir to combine. Reduce the heat to low and cook for 15 minutes, stirring occasionally with a wooden spoon. Remove from the heat and set aside.
5. **To make the sfincione:** Preheat the oven to 400°F (200°C). In a small bowl, combine the bread crumbs, 2 tablespoons of the cheese, oregano, and black pepper.
6. Arrange the anchovy fillets over the dough. Top the anchovies with the remaining 1 cup (100 g) cheese, then the sauce, leaving a 1-inch (2.5 cm) border all the way around. Sprinkle the bread crumb mixture over the top and lightly press the entire sfincione with your fingers, creating indentations to hold the olive oil. Drizzle the olive oil over the top. Bake until the bottom of the crust is golden brown, 30 to 45 minutes.

Nonna Romana Scidurlo's

SPAGHETTI AL PRIMITIVO

SPAGHETTI IN WINE SAUCE

Prep time: 10 minutes
Cook time: 15 minutes
Yield: 4 to 6 servings

Nonna Romana makes this unique pasta dish a few times a year, which I think is perfect for a romantic night in. The pasta is quickly plunged in boiling water and then finishes cooking in a sauce made with garlic, oil, red pepper flakes, and Primitivo wine, a slightly sweet wine from Puglia made with Zinfandel grapes. The spaghetti takes on a lovely reddish-purple tint, and the aroma is undeniably romantic.

- 1 teaspoon salt, plus more for boiling the pasta
- 16 ounces (455 g) dried spaghetti
- ¼ cup (60 ml) extra-virgin olive oil
- 4 cloves garlic, sliced
- ¼ teaspoon red pepper flakes
- 2 cups (480 ml) Primitivo wine or your favorite red wine
- 2 fresh basil leaves, torn , plus more for garnishing

1. Bring a medium pot of salted water to a boil over high heat. Drop in the spaghetti. Cook until pliable, about 5 minutes.
2. Meanwhile, in a large skillet over medium-high heat, add the olive oil, garlic, and red pepper flakes. Cook until the garlic is fragrant and golden, about 2 minutes. Add the wine and bring to a boil over high heat.
3. Using a skimmer, quickly scoop the spaghetti out of the water and transfer it to the skillet, along with ½ cup (120 ml) of the pasta cooking water. (Do not drain the pasta, as you may need to add more pasta cooking water to the pan.)
4. Stir in the basil and the 1 teaspoon of salt. Cook, tossing the pasta in the wine sauce, until the alcohol evaporates and the pasta is al dente, 6 to 7 minutes. If the pan gets a bit dry, add more pasta water, ¼ cup (60 ml) at a time, as needed. Taste and season with salt as desired. Garnish with more basil and serve immediately.

Nonna Dorotea Cristino's

PROFITEROLES CON CREMA DI CIOCCOLATO

CREAM PUFFS WITH CHOCOLATE SAUCE

Prep time: 20 minutes
Cook time: 50 minutes
Yield: 6 to 8 servings

Though the origin of the *profiterole* is French, it is quite popular in Italian cuisine. Nonna Dorotea has always loved making them with her mother-in-law's recipe and filling them with simple Pastry Cream (page 6). She began topping them with a chocolate ganache sauce to take them to the next level, because what's more romantic than chocolate?

CREAM PUFFS

½ cup plus 2 tablespoons (140 g) unsalted butter

Pinch salt

1½ cups (180 g) all-purpose flour

5 large eggs, at room temperature

1 Pastry Cream recipe (page 6)

CHOCOLATE SAUCE

6 ounces (170 g) good-quality dark chocolate, broken into small pieces

¾ cup (180 ml) heavy cream

1 teaspoon vanilla extract

2 tablespoons unsalted butter, softened

1. **To make the cream puffs:** In a large saucepan over medium heat, bring 1 cup (240 ml) of water, the butter, and salt to a boil, then turn off the heat. Little by little, with a wooden spoon, stir in the flour until it is completely absorbed and a dough that pulls away from the edges of the pan forms. Remove the pan from the heat and let cool to room temperature, 10 to 15 minutes.
2. Preheat the oven to 350°F (180°C). Line a baking sheet with parchment paper.
3. One at a time, stir the eggs into the dough until each one is fully incorporated. Transfer the dough to a resealable plastic bag and snip off a lower corner.
4. On the prepared baking sheet, pipe 1-inch (2.5 cm) balls, spacing them 1 inch (2.5 cm) apart. Dip your finger in water and smooth out any sharp points on the dough. Bake until the cream puffs are golden and hollow inside, 20 to 30 minutes. Set on a wire rack to cool completely.
5. Slice the cream puffs in half horizontally and spoon on the pastry cream or pipe it on with a pastry bag.
6. **To make the chocolate sauce:** Place the chopped chocolate in a small heatproof bowl. In a small saucepan over medium-high heat, bring the heavy cream and vanilla to a boil. Pour the hot cream over the chocolate and let stand for 2 minutes. Whisk until the chocolate is completely melted. Add the butter and whisk until the mixture is smooth and shiny.
7. **To assemble:** Dip the bottom of the filled cream puffs into the warm chocolate and arrange on a plate. Drizzle more chocolate over the top of the cream puffs.

Nonna Gilda Castiello Taormina's

CUORI DI PASTA FROLLA ALLA NOCCIOLA

HAZELNUT HEARTS

Prep time: 2 hours 20 minutes
Cook time: 10 minutes
Yield: About 24 cookies

½ cup (58 g) chopped hazelnuts

1 cup (2 sticks/240 g) unsalted butter, at room temperature

⅔ cup (130 g) sugar

2 teaspoons vanilla extract

2 large egg yolks, at room temperature

2 cups (240 g) all-purpose or 00 flour

1 cup (240 ml) Nutella or your favorite chocolate-hazelnut spread

Sprinkles, for decorating

There are few things better than a heart full of Nutella! Nonna Gilda's hazelnut shortbread cookies are an easy way to show someone you love them. They're also fun to make and decorate with grandchildren.

1. In a food processor fitted with the blade attachment, process the hazelnuts until finely ground, about 2 minutes.
2. In the bowl of a stand mixer fitted with the paddle attachment, combine the butter, sugar, and vanilla. Mix at medium-high speed until fluffy, about 5 minutes. With the mixer at low speed, add the ground hazelnuts and mix until incorporated. One at a time, add the egg yolks, mixing at low speed until each yolk is fully incorporated before adding the next one. Add the flour. Mix again until fully absorbed and a dough forms. Do not overmix. Wrap the dough in plastic wrap and flatten it into a disk. Refrigerate for at least 2 hours or up to 5 days.
3. Preheat the oven to 350°F (180°C). Line a baking sheet with aluminum foil or parchment paper.
4. On a lightly floured surface, roll the dough ¼ inch (6 mm) thick. Using a 3-inch (7.5 cm) heart-shaped cookie cutter, cut out as many hearts as possible and place them on the prepared baking sheet, about 1 inch (2.5 cm) apart. Reroll and cut any scraps. If the dough is too soft, wrap it in the plastic wrap and refrigerate until firm. Freeze the cutout hearts for 10 minutes.
5. Bake for 10 minutes. Set on a wire rack to cool completely.
6. Frost each cookie with the chocolate-hazelnut spread and decorate with sprinkles.

Nonna Rina Pesce's

PANNA COTTA CON AMARENE

PANNA COTTA WITH SOUR CHERRIES

Prep time: 4 hours 15 minutes
Cook time: 10 minutes
Yield: 4 servings

I remember my Zia Rina making this pretty pink dessert when she wanted something impressive but not too fussy. *Panna cotta* is a silky, chilled custard-like dessert. It's elegant, delicious, and comes together in 10 minutes, before being chilled in the refrigerator, so it's the perfect make-ahead dessert. She uses Amarena cherries and their syrup to add a little more sweetness and give the panna cotta its romantic color.

- 2½ teaspoons unflavored gelatin
- 1¼ cups (300 ml) whole milk, divided
- 1½ cups (360 ml) heavy whipping cream
- ¼ cup (50 g) sugar
- ½ teaspoon vanilla extract
- 1 jar (16 ounces/455 g) Amarena cherries

1. In a small bowl, dissolve the gelatin in ¼ cup (60 ml) of the milk. Let sit for 5 minutes. Have an ice bath ready.
2. In a large saucepan over medium heat, whisk together the cream, the remaining 1 cup (240 ml) milk, and the sugar. Cook, whisking constantly, until the mixture is warm. Scald the mixture, but do not boil. Remove from the heat and whisk in the gelatin-milk mixture until fully dissolved and very smooth. Add the vanilla. Measure ¾ cup (180 ml) of syrup from the Amarena cherries and whisk it in, creating a pretty pink hue.
3. Place the saucepan over the prepared ice bath and whisk until the mixture is slightly thickened and resembles heavy cream, about 3 minutes. Distribute it evenly among 4 wine glasses. Cover each glass with plastic wrap and refrigerate until set, about 4 hours.
4. Spoon a few Amarena cherries and more syrup over the top before serving.

CARNEVALE

GOOD FRIDAY

Nonna Romana Sciddurlo's

CHIACCHIERE BARESI

BOW TIE FRITTERS

Prep time: 30 minutes
Cook time: 15 minutes
Yield: About 48 fritters

Chiacchiere, crostoli, scorpelle, angel wings, *i uand, frappe*, twists: These are just a few names for these delicious strips of fried pastry dough coated in powdered sugar that are traditionally made for Carnevale. The recipes may vary slightly from region to region, but alcohol always makes an appearance in the dough to give the strips their signature bubbles. Using a pasta roller allows you to make a large quantity for your holiday party, and you'll need them, because these go fast!

½ cup (120 ml) dry white wine, such as Pinot Grigio

2 tablespoons olive oil, plus more for frying

2 tablespoons granulated sugar

1½ cups (180 g) all-purpose or 00 flour

Confectioners' sugar, for dusting

1. In the bowl of a stand mixer fitted with the dough hook attachment, combine the wine, olive oil, and granulated sugar. Mix at medium speed until the sugar dissolves. Add the flour, then mix at medium speed until a supple dough forms, 3 to 5 minutes. Shape the dough into a ball and cover it with plastic wrap. Let rest on the counter for 20 minutes.
2. Working one at a time, flatten a golf ball–size piece of dough between your hands and feed it through the widest setting of a pasta roller 2 or 3 times, folding it until you get an even rectangle without any holes. Then pass them through a #3 setting 2 or 3 times, until you have smooth rectangular sheets. Alternatively, roll the dough with a rolling pin to ⅛-inch (3 mm) thickness.
3. Place the dough sheets on a clean work surface. Using a ravioli cutter, cut out strips of dough about 3 to 4 inches (7.5 to 10 cm) long and 1 inch (2.5 cm) wide. Twist each strip of dough once or twice and press down lightly on the centers.
4. Line a plate with paper towels and set aside. Heat about 2 inches (5 cm) of olive oil in a large heavy-bottomed skillet over high heat. Working in batches, fry the fritters until golden brown, 1 to 2 minutes per batch. Transfer to the paper towel–lined plate and dust with confectioners' sugar.

Nonna Rosa Carmelo's

FIGHI MANDORLATI

BAKED FIGS WITH ALMONDS

Prep time: 15 minutes

Cook time: 2 hours

Yield: 13 baked figs

14 ounces (400 g) whole dried figs (about 26 medium figs), hard stems removed

26 whole raw almonds

Peel of 1 lemon, cut into 26 (½-inch, or 13 mm) pieces

When Nonna Romana and Zia Rosa were little girls in Mola di Bari, they looked forward to Carnevale all year long because it meant that they would be allowed sweets. These baked figs filled with almonds and lemon zest took the place of candy for many children of that generation.

1. Preheat the oven to 200°F (93°C).
2. With a sharp knife, halve the figs horizontally, about three-fourths of the way through, butterflying them so each fig resembles the number 8. Arrange half of the figs, cut sides up.
3. Place 1 whole almond on one cut side of a fig, and 1 piece of lemon zest on the other cut side. Top with a butterflied fig, cut side down. Continue with the remaining figs, almonds, and lemon zest. Arrange the figs on a baking sheet.
4. Bake until the figs turn a slightly darker brown color and have hardened, about 2 hours. Cool to room temperature before eating.

Nonna Rosa Says

To store the figs, my mother, Regina, would layer them in a big clay pot with lots of bay leaves. The aroma brings back memories, even to this day. You can store these in any container you like, but don't forget the bay leaves!

Nonna Gilda Castiello Taormina's

MIGLIACCIO NAPOLETANO

NEAPOLITAN RICOTTA AND SEMOLINA CAKE

Prep time: 20 minutes
Cook time: 1 hour 20 minutes
Yield: 10 to 12 servings

The cousin to the ricotta cheesecake is the Neapolitan *migliaccio* that Nonna Gilda prepares every Carnevale, especially on the day before Ash Wednesday. Coarse semolina is cooked in milk and added to ricotta whipped with eggs to make a light, delicious ricotta cake slightly reminiscent of *sfogliatella* filling.

2 cups (480 ml) whole milk

3 tablespoons unsalted butter, plus more for greasing

1½ cups (300 g) granulated sugar, divided

Zest of 1 lemon

Pinch salt

1 cup (170 g) semolina (not semolina flour)

All-purpose or 00 flour, for dusting

4 large eggs, at room temperature

1½ cups (375 g) whole-milk ricotta

2 teaspoons vanilla extract

¼ cup (36 g) finely diced citron (optional)

Confectioners' sugar, for dusting

1. In a large saucepan over medium heat, bring the milk, butter, ¾ cup (150 g) of the sugar, the lemon zest, salt, and 2 cups (480 ml) of water to a simmer and whisk until the butter melts. Reduce the heat to low.
2. While whisking, add the semolina in a stream, whisking constantly to prevent lumps from forming. (If any lumps should form, smooth them out with a handheld electric mixer afterward.) Continue whisking until the mixture thickens, 3 to 4 minutes. Transfer to a shallow baking dish and spread evenly. Let cool for 15 minutes.
3. Preheat the oven to 365°F (185°C). Grease a 10-inch (25 cm) springform pan with butter and flour the pan.
4. In a large bowl, whisk together the eggs and remaining ¾ cup (150 g) sugar. Add the ricotta and vanilla. Using a handheld electric mixer, mix at high speed until very smooth. Gradually add the cooled semolina-milk mixture and mix at high speed until smooth. Fold in the citron (if using). Pour the mixture into the prepared pan.
5. Bake until the center has set and the cake just begins to turn golden, 1 hour and 10 minutes to 1 hour and 15 minutes. Let cool to room temperature. Dust with confectioners' sugar before cutting.

Nonna Gilda Says

If you find that the top of the cake is browning too quickly, 40 to 50 minutes into baking, cover the top with aluminum foil and continue baking.

Nonna Cecilia Debellis'

ZEPPOLE CON ZUCCHERO E CANNELLA

CINNAMON AND SUGAR ZEPPOLE

Prep time: 30 minutes
Cook time: 45 minutes
Yield: About 30 zeppole

In Italy, Carnevale, or Mardi Gras, is celebrated the forty days before Lent, and usually includes lots of treats fried to perfection. Nonna Cecilia loves making these *zeppole* for *Martedi Grasso* (Fat Tuesday), the day that precedes Ash Wednesday and marks the beginning of Lent. Nonna Cecilia's secret when making zeppole is boiled potatoes, which make the dough pillowy and soft, just the way her mother taught her. With a quick roll in cinnamon sugar after they're fried, these are delicious enough to make year-round.

1 pound (455 g) Yukon Gold potatoes, peeled and halved
3 large eggs, at room temperature
½ cup (120 ml) vegetable oil
1 teaspoon active dry yeast
3⅓ cups (400 g) all-purpose or 00 flour, plus more for dusting
Olive oil, for frying
½ cup (100 g) sugar
1 tablespoon ground cinnamon

1. In a small pot, add the potatoes and enough cold water to cover completely. Bring to a boil over high heat and cook until fork-tender, 15 to 20 minutes. Drain the potatoes and immediately rice them into a medium bowl. Cool for 5 minutes.
2. In the bowl of a stand mixer, add the eggs, vegetable oil, and yeast; let stand for 3 minutes. Attach the dough hook attachment and mix at medium speed until combined. Add the riced potatoes and flour and mix at medium speed until the flour is absorbed and a soft dough forms, 3 to 5 minutes. Cover the bowl with plastic wrap and let rest in a warm place for 30 minutes.
3. Flour your hands. Take a golf ball-size chunk of dough and roll it into a ½-inch-thick (13 mm) rope, 8 to 10 inches (20 to 25 cm) long. Twist the rope twice and place it on a baking sheet. Continue rolling and forming twists with the remaining dough.
4. Line a large plate with paper towels. Heat 2 inches (5 cm) of olive oil in a small pot over high heat. Working in batches, carefully drop the zeppole into the hot oil, 2 or 3 at a time, and fry until golden brown, 2 to 3 minutes per batch, then transfer to the prepared plate.
5. In a shallow dish, whisk together the sugar and cinnamon. Roll the zeppole in the sugar-cinnamon mixture while still warm and serve.

Nonna Romana Sciddurlo's

CECI FRITTI

OVEN-FRIED CHICKPEAS

Prep time: 15 minutes, plus 12 hours soaking

Cook time: 35 minutes

Yield: 6 to 8 servings

16 ounces (455 g) dried chickpeas

2 teaspoons salt

12 bay leaves

To celebrate Carnevale in Italy, many families would throw fun costume parties in the home and serve humble treats like these oven-fried chickpeas. They are delightfully crunchy, and they double as a healthy snack.

1. In a medium saucepan, combine the chickpeas, salt, and bay leaves. Cover with enough cold water to come up 3 inches (7.5 cm) above the chickpeas. Soak for 12 hours.
2. Preheat the oven to 400°F (200° C).
3. Drain and pat the chickpeas dry with a clean kitchen towel. Spread the chickpeas in an even layer on a baking sheet. Bake until the chickpeas are golden brown, 35 minutes.

Nonna Rosa Carmelo's

SCALCIONE

SAVORY SCALLION PIE

Prep time: 10 minutes
Cook time: 1 hour 15 minutes
Yield: 4 to 6 servings

FILLING

6 bunches scallions (35 to 40 stalks)

¼ cup (60 ml) extra-virgin olive oil

½ cup (128 g) canned crushed tomatoes or 1 cup (150 g) cherry tomatoes, halved

1 cup (192 g) pitted Gaeta or Kalamata olives

½ cup (120 ml) dry white wine, such as Pinot Grigio or Sauvignon Blanc

5 anchovy fillets, broken up into small pieces (optional)

CRUST

⅓ cup (80 ml) extra-virgin olive oil, plus more for greasing and brushing

1 cup (240 ml) dry white wine, such as Pinot Grigio or Sauvignon Blanc

1 teaspoon salt

3⅓ cups (400 g) all-purpose or 00 flour, plus more for dusting

Every Good Friday, families from Puglia enjoy a pie crust made with white wine, oil, and flour, and stuffed with an onion filling that varies from village to village. My Zia Rosa's is by far the best in the family. We all love it so much that she makes it throughout the year.

1. **To make the filling:** Trim the green ends of the scallions. With a paring knife, split the bulbs of the scallions in half lengthwise. Cut the scallions into 1½-inch (4 cm) pieces. Wash them well under cold water.
2. In a small pot, heat the oil over medium-high heat. Add the scallions, tomatoes, olives, and wine and stir with a wooden spoon. Cover and cook until the scallions are soft, about 15 minutes. Remove from the heat and transfer to a colander with a plate underneath to drain the juice. Set aside until cool.
3. **Meanwhile, make the crust:** Preheat the oven to 400°F (200°C). Grease a 12-inch (30 cm) round pizza pan with olive oil.
4. In the bowl of a stand mixer fitted with the dough hook attachment, combine the olive oil, wine, and salt, and mix for 30 seconds at low speed. Add the flour and mix until a smooth dough forms, 2 to 3 minutes.
5. Turn out the dough onto a lightly floured surface. Halve the dough and roll one half into a 14-inch (36 cm) circle. Roll the dough around the rolling pin and unfurl it over the prepared pan. Smooth the sides and fit the dough into the corners of the pan, allowing the excess to come up the sides. Add the scallion filling to the center of the crust and spread it evenly, leaving a border of about ½ inch (12 mm). Place the pieces of anchovy (if using) over the scallions.
6. Roll out the remaining dough into another 14-inch (36 cm) circle. Place it over the scallions and press the top and bottom crusts together with your fingers. Trim any excess dough from the top. Press the border of the crust with the tines of a fork to create a seal. Brush the crust with olive oil and dock all over with a fork. Bake until the crust has colored, about 1 hour. Serve warm or at room temperature.

Nonna Maria Fiore's

PASTICCIO DI TONNO

TUNA PIE WITH TOMATOES AND PARSLEY

Prep time: 1 hour 30 minutes

Cook time: 1 hour 5 minutes

Yield: 6 to 8 servings

Variations of this meatless pie are served all over the Puglia region of Italy to break the Good Friday fast. Nonna Maria's version features a light, pillowy crust that is typical of her village of Altamura. Since this pie has so few ingredients, it's imperative to use quality products. Nonna Maria loves canned tuna packed in oil and imported from Italy, which she finds at Italian specialty stores in Brooklyn.

DOUGH

4 cups (680 g) semolina bread flour

2 teaspoons salt

1¾ cups (420 ml) warm water

2 packets (¼ ounce/7 g each) active dry yeast

FILLING

2 cans (5 ounces/42 g each) yellowtail tuna, packed in olive oil, drained (if you cannot find yellowtail, use any tuna you like as long as it's packed in oil)

½ cup (120 ml) extra-virgin olive oil

6 cloves garlic, minced

2 cups (120 g) fresh parsley leaves

1½ cups (225 g) cherry tomatoes

½ teaspoon salt

ASSEMBLY

¼ cup (60 ml) extra-virgin olive oil, divided

1. **To make the dough:** On a clean work surface, combine the flour and the salt. Make a well in the center and add the warm water and yeast. Let sit until bubbles begin to form, 3 to 5 minutes.
2. Using your fingers, incorporate the flour into the water. Knead until a supple dough forms, 8 to 10 minutes. Wrap the dough in a clean kitchen towel and let rest in a warm place until doubled in size, about 1 hour.
3. **Meanwhile, make the filling:** In a medium bowl, break up the tuna with a fork.
4. In a medium pan with a lid, heat the olive oil over medium heat. Add the garlic and cook, stirring occasionally, until brown, about 2 minutes. Add the parsley, cover the pan, and cook until it wilts, about 2 minutes. Add the tomatoes and the salt. Reduce the heat to medium-low, cover the pan, and cook until the tomatoes break down, 10 to 15 minutes. Remove from the heat and transfer to a medium bowl. Mix in the tuna. Set aside.
5. **To assemble:** Preheat the oven to 350°F (180°C). Drizzle a baking sheet with 2 tablespoons of the olive oil.
6. Turn out the dough onto a work surface and knead it for 2 to 3 minutes. Cut the dough in half. Using a rolling pin, roll out one half into a rectangle as thin as you can get it and larger than the baking sheet. Roll the dough onto the rolling pin and transfer it to the prepared baking sheet. Let any excess hang over the sides. Spread the tuna filling over the dough in an even layer, leaving a 1-inch (2.5 cm) border on all sides.

7 Roll out the second piece of dough to the same size and cover the filling with it. Trim any excess to the top of the pan, about 1 inch (2.5 cm). Fold the excess bottom dough over and press firmly with your fingers. Press the edges with the tines of a fork to seal. Brush the top with the remaining 2 tablespoons (30 ml) olive oil and dock all over with a fork.

8 Bake until the top of the pie is golden, 40 to 45 minutes. Cool to room temperature, cut into slices, and serve.

Nonna Maria Says

Every time I leave dough to rise, I say a little prayer my mother always used to say to ensure a good levitation: "*Cresci pane, cresci pasta come cresceva Gesu' bambino nella fascia.*"

EASTER DAY

EASTER DAY

LITTLE EASTER

LITTLE EASTER

Nonna Romana Sciddurlo's

TIELLA DI AGNELLO E PATATE

LAMB WITH POTATOES

Prep time: 15 minutes
Cook time: 1 hour 15 minutes
Yield: 4 to 6 servings

If you're entertaining a big group for Easter (yes, I know this is an Italian holiday cookbook and the idea of entertaining anything but a big group is silly), and you want to make an easy but impressive entrée, then look no further than this dish, which is prepared in the true Pugliese fashion with super-simple ingredients that won't compete with the flavor of the lamb. Nonna Romana says she loves this dish because the potatoes and tomatoes are a built-in side dish of sorts and are very satisfying. If you want to be very traditional, bake this in a terra-cotta pot, which conducts heat beautifully and cooks the meat evenly; otherwise, any large baking pan will do the job.

- 2 pounds (910 g) lamb, mixed cuts or your preferred cut
- Salt and black pepper
- 5 medium russet potatoes, scrubbed, peeled, and sliced into ¼-inch-thick (6 mm) rounds
- 2 cups (300 g) cherry tomatoes, halved
- 1 medium red or white onion, cut into 1-inch (2.5 cm) dice
- 10 small fresh rosemary sprigs
- 3 or 4 bay leaves
- ¼ teaspoon red pepper flakes
- ¾ cup (180 ml) white wine, such as Pinot Grigio or Chablis
- ¼ cup (60 ml) extra-virgin olive oil
- 3 tablespoons grated Pecorino Romano cheese

1. Preheat the oven to 400°F (200°C).
2. Season the lamb well with salt and pepper. (Lamb tends not to absorb salt as well, so you might want to add a little more than you think you need.)
3. In a large bowl, combine the potatoes, tomatoes (reserve a few for squeezing on top), onion, rosemary, bay leaves, red pepper flakes, and season with salt as desired. Add the wine, olive oil, and the lamb and mix until well incorporated. Transfer to a baking sheet or a terra-cotta pot, spreading everything into an even layer. Sprinkle the cheese over the entire surface, particularly over the potatoes. Squeeze the reserved tomatoes with your hands over the potatoes and sprinkle them over the top.
4. Bake until the potatoes have colored nicely and an instant-read meat thermometer inserted into the lamb reads between 145°F (63°C) for medium-rare and 160°F (71°C) for medium, 1 hour to 1 hour and 15 minutes. Remove the bay leaves before serving.

Nonna Annita Fallone Apruzzese's

CONIGLIO CON PANCETTA E VERDURE

RABBIT WITH PANCETTA AND VEGETABLES

Prep time: 1 hour 15 minutes

Cook time: 1 hour 15 minutes

Yield: 4 servings

For Nonna Annita, rabbit is a comfort food of sorts, as it reminds her of growing up in Ciociaria, where rabbit is part of the local culinary tradition. She only began using carrots in this dish when she arrived in America because she said there were none when she was growing up in Italy.

1 rabbit (2½ pounds/1.1 kg), fresh or frozen and thawed (see Nonna Annita Says)

Cold water, as needed

1 cup (240 ml) white wine vinegar

3 tablespoons extra-virgin olive oil

4 ounces (113 g) pancetta, cut into ¼-inch (6 mm) dice

2 small carrots, cut into 1½-inch (4 cm) pieces

2 shallots, cut into ¼-inch (6 mm) dice

1 rib celery, cut into 1½-inch (4 cm) pieces

2 bay leaves

2 to 3 fresh rosemary sprigs

1 teaspoon salt, divided

½ teaspoon black pepper, divided

1 cup (240 ml) dry white wine, such as Pinot Grigio

1. Place the rabbit in a large bowl and cover it with cold water. Add the vinegar and let soak for 1 hour to remove any gaminess. Drain and pat dry.
2. Heat a large heavy-bottomed skillet with a lid over high heat. Add the rabbit to the dry skillet and sear, turning frequently with tongs to draw out the water, 3 to 5 minutes. Transfer to a plate or bowl. Discard the water and clean the skillet.
3. In the cleaned skillet, heat the olive oil over medium-high heat. Add the pancetta. Cook and stir until crisp, about 5 minutes. With a slotted spoon, transfer to a medium bowl, leaving the fat in the skillet.
4. Return the skillet to the heat and add the carrots, shallots, celery, bay leaves, and rosemary. Cook, stirring occasionally, until the shallots are translucent and the vegetables are soft, 7 to 9 minutes. Season with about half the salt and pepper and transfer the vegetables to the bowl with the pancetta.
5. Return the skillet to the heat and add the rabbit and its juices. Increase the heat to high. Cook, turning frequently, until the rabbit develops some color, 5 to 7 minutes. Season with the remaining salt and pepper. Add the wine to the skillet and scrape up any browned bits from the bottom. Cook for 2 to 3 minutes. Add the vegetables and pancetta to the skillet and reduce the heat to low. Cover the skillet and cook until the rabbit is tender and most of the liquid has reduced, 40 to 45 minutes. Remove the bay leaves and rosemary sprigs before serving.

Nonna Annita Says

Ask your butcher to cut up the rabbit as follows: Remove and discard the kidneys, liver, and heart. Cut the front legs from the backbone, cut out the hind legs, and cut the saddle into 2 pieces.

Nonna Teresa Petruccelli-Formato's

RIGATONI AL FORNO CON VERDURE

BAKED RIGATONI WITH SPRING VEGETABLES

Prep time: 30 minutes

Cook time: 1 hour 35 minutes

Yield: 6 to 8 servings

There's no better way to welcome spring than with this pasta dish! It's perfect for holiday meals because you can fully assemble it and leave it in the fridge the night before. Just let it come to room temperature before baking, and you're good to go.

SAUCE

3 tablespoons extra-virgin olive oil, divided

1 small onion, cut into 2-inch (5 cm) slices

4 cloves garlic, sliced

12 ounces (340 g) mini sweet peppers, cut into ¼-inch (6 mm) strips

1 medium zucchini, cut into 1-inch (2.5 cm) chunks

1 medium eggplant, skin on, cut into 2-inch (5 cm) chunks

2 teaspoons salt, divided, plus more to taste

1 can (28 ounces/794 g) crushed tomatoes

¼ cup (10 g) chopped fresh basil

PASTA

Salt

16 ounces (455 g) dried rigatoni pasta

16 ounces (455 g) mozzarella cheese, shredded, divided

⅔ cup (67 g) grated Parmigiano-Reggiano cheese, divided

1. **To make the sauce:** Heat 2 tablespoons of the olive oil in a large heavy-bottomed skillet over medium heat. Add the onion, garlic, and peppers and cook, stirring occasionally, until the onion is translucent and the peppers soften, 10 to 12 minutes. Add the zucchini and cook, stirring occasionally, until soft, 8 to 10 minutes. Add the remaining 1 tablespoon olive oil, the eggplant, and 1 teaspoon of the salt. Cook, stirring occasionally with a wooden spoon, until the eggplant softens, 5 to 7 minutes. Stir in the tomatoes, basil, the remaining 1 teaspoon salt, and 1 cup (240 ml) of water. Reduce the heat to low, cover the skillet, and cook for 10 to 12 minutes. Scoop out and reserve 2 cups (480 ml) of sauce.
2. Preheat the oven to 350°F (180°C).
3. **To make the pasta:** Bring a medium stockpot of generously salted water to a boil over medium-high heat. Drop in the pasta and cook for half the time listed on the package instructions, about 6 minutes. You want the pasta to be very al dente. Drain and run the pasta under cold water, then add it to the remaining vegetable sauce in the skillet. Toss to coat evenly.
4. **To assemble:** Spread 1 cup (240 ml) of the reserved sauce on the bottom of a 9 by 13-inch (23 by 33 cm) baking dish. Add half of the pasta and top it with half of the mozzarella and half of the Parmigiano-Reggiano. Add the remaining pasta, spreading it into an even layer, and top it with the remaining reserved sauce, the remaining mozzarella, and the remaining Parmigiano-Reggiano.
5. Bake until the cheese melts and the top pieces of pasta are slightly charred, 35 to 45 minutes. Serve immediately.

Nonna Rosa Carmelo's

PAPPARDELLE CON RAGÙ DI AGNELLO E RICOTTA

PAPPARDELLE WITH LAMB RAGÙ AND WHIPPED RICOTTA

Prep time: 20 minutes
Cook time: 1 hour
Yield: 4 to 6 servings

On Sundays, Italians have sauce—even on Easter Sunday. This is the perfect first course for Easter Sunday, and the hearty meat sauce is full of flavor and comes together quickly. Try not to skip the mint leaves, which complement the lamb beautifully.

- 3 tablespoons extra-virgin olive oil
- 1 medium carrot, cut into ¼-inch (6 mm) dice
- 1 stalk celery, cut into ¼-inch (6 mm) dice
- 1 large shallot, cut into ¼-inch (6 mm) dice
- ½ teaspoon red pepper flakes
- 1 pound (455 g) ground lamb
- 1 pound (455 g) lamb neck bones
- 2 bay leaves
- 2 fresh rosemary sprigs, chopped
- 2 fresh thyme sprigs, chopped
- Salt and black pepper
- 1 cup (240 ml) dry red wine, such as Merlot
- 3 tablespoons tomato paste
- 1 can (28 ounces/794 g) crushed tomatoes
- 16 ounces (455 g) dried pappardelle pasta
- 1 cup (100 g) grated Pecorino Romano cheese
- 2 cups (500 g) whole-milk ricotta
- 8 to 10 fresh mint leaves, for garnish

1. Heat the olive oil in a large Dutch oven or cast-iron pot over medium heat. Add the carrot, celery, shallot, and red pepper flakes. Increase the heat to high and cook, stirring occasionally, until soft, 7 to 10 minutes.
2. Add the ground lamb, the bones, bay leaves, rosemary, and thyme. Season with salt and pepper. Cook, stirring occasionally, until the lamb is nicely browned, 5 to 7 minutes.
3. Add the wine; cook until it evaporates, about 5 minutes. Add the tomato paste and the tomatoes. Bring the mixture to a boil, then reduce the heat to a simmer. Cover the pot and cook for 10 minutes.
4. Uncover the pot and simmer until the sauce is reduced, about 20 minutes. Remove and discard the bones and bay leaves.
5. Bring a medium stockpot of salted water to a boil. Add the pasta and cook until al dente.
6. Meanwhile, make the whipped ricotta. In a food processor or blender, blend the ricotta for about 20 seconds. Set aside.
7. Transfer the sauce to a large bowl. Drain the pasta and add it to the sauce; toss to combine. Add the Pecorino Romano and toss again, allowing the residual heat of the pasta to melt the cheese. Serve in warm bowls topped with a dollop of whipped ricotta and garnished with mint leaves.

Nonna Angelina Purpura's

AGNELLO AGRODOLCE

SWEET-AND-SOUR LAMB

Prep time: 10 minutes
Cook time: 55 minutes
Yield: 6 to 8 servings

You will absolutely want to make Nonna Angelina's sweet-and-sour lamb for your next Easter dinner. This dish is bursting with exuberant flavors and textures that represent Sicily: sweet, sour, and crunchy. She sears the lamb to perfection in a pan with plenty of onion, then cooks it in a wine and vinegar emulsion before topping it with sugared almonds for some delicious crunch.

½ cup (72 g) whole raw almonds

2 pounds (910 g) lamb, any cut, as long as the pieces are about 1 inch (2.5 cm) thick

Salt and black pepper

½ cup (120 ml) extra-virgin olive oil

1 large onion, sliced

1 cup (240 ml) dry white wine, such as Pinot Grigio

¼ cup (50 g) plus 1 teaspoon sugar, divided

¼ cup (60 ml) red wine vinegar

1. Preheat the oven to 400°F (200°C).
2. Spread the almonds on a baking sheet and toast them in the oven for 10 minutes. Remove, coarsely chop, and set aside.
3. Season the lamb well with salt and pepper. (Lamb tends not to absorb salt as well, so you might want to add a little more salt than you think you need.)
4. In a large skillet, heat the olive oil over medium-high heat. Add the lamb. Sear all over, 2 to 3 minutes per side. Transfer to a plate. Add the onion to the skillet and cook, stirring occasionally until soft and slightly golden, 2 to 3 minutes. Return the lamb to the skillet, along with any juices. Cook for 2 to 3 minutes. Add the wine and stir to loosen any browned bits from the bottom of the skillet. Reduce the heat to medium-low, cover the pan, and cook for 20 to 25 minutes.
5. In a small bowl, toss together the chopped toasted almonds and 1 teaspoon of the sugar.
6. In another small bowl, stir together the vinegar and remaining ¼ cup (50 g) sugar. Add the vinegar and sugar mixture to the skillet and cook, stirring occasionally, for 5 minutes.
7. Transfer the lamb to a serving plate and sprinkle with the sugared almonds. Serve at room temperature.

Nonna Romana Sciddurlo's

PIZZA RUSTICA

Prep time: 50 minutes

Cook time: 1 hour 15 minutes

Yield: 6 to 8 servings

DOUGH

3⅓ cups (400 g) all-purpose or 00 flour, plus more for dusting

Dash salt

1 cup (2 sticks/240 g) cold unsalted butter, cubed, plus more for greasing

3 large eggs

¼ cup (60 ml) whole milk, plus more as necessary

FILLING

4 ounces (113 g) prosciutto, cut into ½-inch (13 mm) cubes

4 ounces (113 g) sopressata, cut into ½-inch (13 mm) cubes

4 ounces (113 g) mortadella, cut into ½-inch (13 mm) cubes

4 ounces (113 g) fresh mozzarella cheese, cut into ½-inch (13 mm) cubes

4 ounces (113 g) sharp provolone cheese, cut into ½-inch (13 mm) cubes

¼ cup (25 g) grated Pecorino Romano cheese

3 large eggs

16 ounces (455 g) basket cheese, cut into ½-inch (13 mm) cubes

Black pepper

This rich, decadent recipe is the perfect mix of cheeses and meats baked together in a flaky pastry dough that Italians usually serve to break the Lenten fast for the Easter holidays.

1. **To make the crust:** In the bowl of a stand mixer fitted with the dough hook attachment, combine the flour, salt, and butter. Start at low speed, then increase the speed to high and mix until all of the flour is absorbed.
2. With the mixer at low speed, add 2 of the eggs, one at a time, mixing until they are fully incorporated. Add the milk and mix until a ball of dough forms. (If the dough seems a bit dry, add another tablespoon of milk.) Mix at medium speed until the dough is supple, about 10 minutes. Wrap the dough in plastic wrap and refrigerate for 30 minutes.
3. **Meanwhile, make the filling:** In a large bowl, combine the prosciutto, sopressata, mortadella, mozzarella, provolone, and Pecorino, and mix well. Add the 3 eggs and mix well, making sure everything is evenly coated. Add the basket cheese and mix gently so as not to break it apart too much. Season with fresh black pepper.
4. **To assemble:** Preheat the oven to 350°F (175°C). Grease a 9-inch (23 cm) springform pan with butter and dust it with flour.
5. Transfer two-thirds of the dough to a lightly floured work surface. Wrap the remaining dough in plastic wrap and refrigerate until ready to use. Using a lightly floured rolling pin, roll out the dough to a 16-inch (41 cm) circle, about ¼ inch (6mm) thick. Roll the dough onto the rolling pin and unfurl it over the pan and up the sides, letting the excess hang over the sides. Add the filling and spread it into an even layer. With a sharp knife, trim the excess dough.
6. On a lightly floured work surface, combine the scraps with the remaining one-third of dough and roll it out ¼ inch (6 mm) thick. With a ravioli cutter, cut the dough into 1½-inch (4 cm) strips and place them in a lattice pattern over the filling; press the edges slightly to adhere. Trim any excess dough.
7. In a small bowl, beat the remaining egg with 1 tablespoon of water. Brush the lattice top with the egg wash. Bake until the center is set and the crust is nicely colored, about 1 hour and 15 minutes. Let cool completely before serving.

Nonna Teresa Petruccelli-Formato's

QUAGLIE ALLA CACCIATORA

HUNTER'S–STYLE QUAIL

Prep time: 15 minutes
Cook time: 45 minutes
Yield: 4 to 6 servings

"My kids loved quail growing up! They used to fight over the little legs because those always had the most meat," Nonna Teresa says of her quail cooked in a delicious hunter's-style sauce. This dish is usually made with chicken, but quail is a wonderful alternative; its dark flesh is well matched with the rich flavors of the sauce.

- 2 pounds (910 g) quail, about 6 small birds
- Salt and black pepper
- 3 tablespoons extra-virgin olive oil
- 2 cloves garlic, halved
- ¼ cup (60 ml) brandy
- 2 tablespoons grappa
- ¼ cup (60 ml) dry white wine, such as Pinot Grigio
- 10 ounces (280 g) cremini mushrooms, sliced
- 1 medium onion, sliced into half-moons
- 2 cups (300 g) cherry tomatoes, halved
- ¼ cup (16 g) chopped fresh parsley
- ½ cup (120 ml) vegetable broth

1. Check for any little feathers still stuck to the quail and pull them off. Using kitchen shears, butterfly each quail by cutting straight along the belly. Cut off any excess fat that hangs off the quail. Discard the necks and any innards. Run the quail under cold water. Pat dry with paper towels and place them on a baking sheet. Season both sides of the quail with salt and pepper.
2. Heat the olive oil in a large heavy-bottomed skillet with a lid over medium-high heat. Add the garlic and cook, stirring occasionally, until the garlic is golden, 1 to 2 minutes. Place the quail in the skillet, cut side down, and sear all over, 3 to 4 minutes per side. Remove the garlic if you like.
3. Reduce the heat to medium. Remove the skillet from the heat, add the brandy, grappa, and wine, then return it to the heat. Cook until the alcohol evaporates, stirring to loosen any browned bits from the bottom of the pan, 2 to 3 minutes. Transfer the quail to a plate.
4. To the skillet, add the mushrooms, onion, tomatoes, and parsley, and season with salt and pepper to taste. Using a wooden spoon, smash the tomatoes. Cook for 4 to 5 minutes. Return the quail to the skillet, along with any juices. Pour in the broth and reduce the heat to low. Cover the skillet and cook for 20 minutes.

Nonna Carmela D'Angelo's

CROSTATA DI BACCALÀ

BACCALÀ PIE

Prep time: 20 minutes, plus 1 to 3 days soaking

Cook time: 40 minutes

Yield: 6 to 8 servings

FILLING

1 pound (455 g) baccalà (salt cod)

Cold water, for soaking

2 tablespoons extra-virgin olive oil

1 medium onion, thinly sliced

½ cup (75 g) raisins

½ cup (96 g) pitted green olives, coarsely chopped

¼ cup (36 g) capers

2 anchovy fillets packed in olive oil

½ teaspoon black pepper

CRUST

⅓ cup (80 ml) extra-virgin olive oil, plus more for greasing and brushing

1 cup (240 ml) dry white wine, such as Pinot Grigio or Sauvignon Blanc

1 teaspoon salt

3⅓ cups (400 g) all-purpose or 00 flour, plus more for dusting

1 large egg beaten with 1 tablespoon water (for egg wash)

Nonna Carmela's baccalà pie uses the traditional Pugliese dough and has a filling that is the perfect blend of sweet and savory. Her grandchildren have taken on the tradition of making these pies every year for Easter.

1. **To make the filling:** In a large bowl, add the baccalà and enough cold water to cover it . Place the bowl in the refrigerator and change the water 3 times a day; repeat for 1 to 3 days, depending on saltiness. Drain the baccalà and shred it by hand into bite-size pieces.
2. In a large skillet, heat the olive oil over medium heat. Add the onion and cook, stirring occasionally, until soft and transparent, 8 to 10 minutes. Add the shredded baccalà, the raisins, olives, capers, anchovies, and black pepper and cook, stirring with a wooden spoon, for 3 to 5 minutes. Remove from the heat and set aside to cool to room temperature.
3. **Meanwhile, make the crust:** In the bowl of a stand mixer fitted with the dough hook attachment, combine the olive oil, wine, and salt; mix at low speed for 30 seconds. Add the flour and mix until a smooth dough forms, 2 to 3 minutes.
4. **To assemble:** Preheat the oven to 425°F (220°C). Grease a 9-inch (23 cm) round pie pan with olive oil.
5. Turn out the dough onto a lightly floured work surface and cut it in half. Roll out one half into a 12-inch (30 cm) circle, about ¼-inch thick (6 mm). Roll the dough onto the rolling pin and unfurl it into the prepared pie pan. Add the cooled filling and spread it into an even layer.
6. Roll out the remaining half of the dough into a 10-inch (25 cm) circle, then transfer it to the top of the pie. Press the edges with your fingers to seal. Trim any excess dough with a sharp knife, then press around the edges with the tines of a fork. Brush the top with the egg wash and dock the crust all over with a fork.
7. Bake until the crust is nicely colored, 35 to 40 minutes.

Nonna Maria Pesce's

ZUCCHINE RIPIENE

STUFFED ZUCCHINI

Prep time: 10 minutes
Cook time: 1 hour 40 minutes
Yield: 4 to 6 servings

Whenever you go to Nonna Maria's house for a holiday meal, there is always something ready for you to snack on. These meat-stuffed zucchini are a lovely springtime appetizer or side dish for holiday entertaining. Nonna Maria hollows out the zucchini to make little cups and fills them with a mixture of sautéed meat and diced zucchini flesh, making them perfect for a dinner party or a buffet.

- 4 to 5 large zucchini (look for zucchini that are nice and wide), cut into 2-inch-thick (5 cm) rounds (about 20)
- 3 tablespoons extra-virgin olive oil, plus more for drizzling
- 1 teaspoon salt, divided
- ¼ teaspoon black pepper
- 6 tablespoons white wine, such as Pinot Grigio, divided
- 1 pound (455 g) ground beef
- 5 tablespoons grated Parmigiano-Reggiano cheese
- ¼ cup (30 g) plain bread crumbs
- 1 large egg, beaten
- 3 tablespoons minced fresh parsley plus 4 or 5 sprigs, divided
- 1 small onion, sliced

1. Preheat the oven to 400°F (200°C).
2. Using a sharp knife, hollow out the center of the zucchini rounds, leaving about ¼ inch (6 mm) on the edges. Chop the zucchini flesh into ¼-inch (6 mm) dice and transfer to a medium skillet. Set aside.
3. Stand the zucchini rounds in a 9 by 13-inch (23 by 33 cm) baking dish. Pour 1¾ cups (420 ml) of water into the bottom of the dish and bake until fork-tender and most of the water has evaporated, 30 to 35 minutes. Remove from the oven and set aside.
4. Put the skillet with the zucchini flesh over medium heat and add the olive oil, ½ teaspoon of the salt, and the pepper. Cook, stirring frequently, for 2 to 3 minutes. Add ¼ cup (60 ml) of the wine. Cook, stirring occasionally, until the zucchini develops some color, 12 to 15 minutes. Using a slotted spoon, transfer the zucchini to a large bowl, reserving the oil in the pan.
5. To the pan, add the ground beef, the remaining 2 tablespoons wine, and remaining ½ teaspoon salt to the skillet. Cook, stirring frequently, until the meat is just browned, 3 to 4 minutes. Remove from the heat. Using a slotted spoon, transfer the meat to the bowl with the sautéed zucchini. Discard the fat in the pan. Let the zucchini-meat mixture cool for 10 minutes. Once cool, stir in in the cheese, bread crumbs, egg, and minced parsley.
6. Place the onion slices and parsley sprigs between the zucchini rounds in the baking dish. Fill each zucchini round with 1½ to 2 tablespoons of filling. Drizzle with a bit of olive oil and bake until the top of the meat is browned, 25 to 30 minutes.

Nonna Antoinette Capodicci's

CASATIELLO NAPOLETANO

NEAPOLITAN EASTER MEAT AND CHEESE RING

Prep time: 4 hours

Cook time: 1 hour

Yield: 10 to 12 servings

DOUGH

5 ounces (140 g) lard, plus more for greasing the pan and dotting the dough

1 packet (¼ ounce/7 g) active dry yeast

1 cup (240 ml) warm water, divided, plus more as needed

½ teaspoon sugar

4 cups (496 g) all-purpose or 00 flour

2 teaspoons salt

1 teaspoon coarsely ground black pepper

FILLING

½ cup (50 g) grated Pecorino Romano cheese

½ cup (50 g) grated Parmigiano-Reggiano cheese

4 ounces (113 g) mortadella or ham, cut into ½-inch (13 mm) dice

4 ounces (113 g) Genoa salami, cut into ½-inch (13 mm) dice

4 ounces (113 g) pancetta, cut into ½-inch (13 mm) dice

4 ounces (113 g) semi-sharp provolone cheese, cut into ½-inch (13 mm) dice

Black pepper

TOPPING

5 large eggs, washed and dried, divided

To most Neapolitans, the *casatiello* is a sacred Easter tradition. A rustic, savory, leavened bread is bathed in lard and filled with meats and cheeses; it carries great religious symbolism for the Easter holiday. The flour that makes the bread signifies the body of Christ, the eggs on top represent new life, and the strips of dough holding the eggs, Jesus' crown of thorns. Even its ring shape symbolizes infinity. Though it possesses great significance, most importantly, the casatiello is absolutely delicious, and Nonna Antoinette's is flawless. This bread is perfect when eaten hot or cold, and any leftovers can and should absolutely be eaten for *la Pasquetta* the day after Easter.

1. **To make the dough:** Grease a 10-inch (25 cm) loose-bottomed tube pan with a little lard and set aside.
2. In a small bowl, combine the yeast with ½ cup (120 ml) of the warm water and the sugar. Let sit until the surface gets foamy, about 5 minutes.
3. On a work surface, place the flour and form a well in the center. Add the yeast mixture, 5 ounces (140 g) of lard, the salt, and the pepper. Gradually work the ingredients into the flour. Add the remaining ½ cup (120 ml) warm water and mix until a soft dough ball forms. If the dough looks dry, add 1 tablespoon of water at a time, until it comes together. Knead until the dough is smooth and elastic.
4. Pinch off a ball of dough (about the size of a tennis ball) and save for later. With a rolling pin, roll the remaining dough into a 14 by 18-inch (36 by 46 cm) rectangle. Dot the dough all over with lard.
5. **To make the filling:** Sprinkle the grated Pecorino and Parmigiano-Reggiano over the dough. Top with the mortadella, salami, pancetta, provolone, and a little pepper. Starting at the long side closest to you, roll the dough jellyroll style, making sure to tuck in the ends. Place it in the prepared pan, tucking the ends together to form a circle. Top the dough with little dots of lard all over. Cover with plastic wrap and let rest in a warm place until the dough has doubled in size, 2 to 3 hours.

CONTINUED ON PAGE 50

CONTINUED FROM PAGE 48

6 Preheat the oven to 375°F (190°C).

7 **To make the topping:** Place 4 of the eggs in their shells randomly on the top of the dough, pressing gently until they are halfway in. Divide the reserved piece of dough into 8 equal pieces. Roll each piece into 4-inch-long (10 cm) ropes. Use 2 pieces to make a cross over each egg, attaching the eggs to the top of the dough.

8 Bake until a toothpick inserted in the center comes out clean, 45 minutes to an hour. When the casatiello has about 15 minutes to go, beat the remaining egg and brush it onto the dough. This will give it a shiny golden-brown color. If the top is getting too dark, loosely cover it with aluminum foil.

9 Transfer to a wire rack to cool. Run a knife along the inside edges of the pan, loosen the bottom, and remove the bread. Cut into slices and serve warm.

Nonna Antoinette Capodicci's

PANE DI PASQUA

SOFT EASTER BREAD

Prep time: 2 hours 40 minutes

Cook time: 25 minutes

Yield: One 1-pound (455 g) Easter bread

Every year, Nonna Antoinette's *nipotini* (grandchildren) look forward to her soft Easter bread, which bakes up fluffy with a wonderfully tender crumb every time. And even though I'm all grown up, there's just something about seeing those pastel-colored Easter eggs in the bread that fills me with wonder. You can make this recipe in a stand mixer, but Nonna Antoinette urges that mixing it by hand on a board the old-fashioned way is the way to go, and Nonna knows best!

BREAD

2/3 cup (160 ml) whole milk

1 packet (1/4 ounce/7 g) active dry yeast

1/2 cup (100 g) granulated sugar, divided

2 3/4 cups (330 g) all-purpose or 00 flour, plus more for dusting

1 teaspoon salt

2 large eggs, at room temperature

3 tablespoons unsalted butter, at room temperature

1 teaspoon lemon extract

1 teaspoon orange extract

Olive oil, for greasing

TOPPING

4 large eggs, dyed (not hard-boiled)

2 large egg yolks, beaten

1/2 cup (60 g) confectioners' sugar

1/4 cup (60 ml) whole milk

1 teaspoon anise extract

Rainbow nonpareils, for decorating

1. **To make the bread:** Line a baking sheet with parchment paper.
2. In a small saucepan over low heat, warm the milk until it is lukewarm. Pour it into a small bowl and stir in the yeast and 1 teaspoon of the granulated sugar. Let stand until the mixture bubbles, about 10 minutes.
3. In a large bowl, whisk together the flour, salt, and the remaining granulated sugar. Make a well in the center and slowly pour the milk mixture into it, stirring gently. Add the eggs, butter, lemon extract, and orange extract. Mix with your hands until a dough begins to come together.
4. Generously flour a work surface and turn the dough out onto it. Knead by hand until it is smooth and elastic; it should be soft and a little sticky. Shape the dough into a ball. Lightly coat a bowl with olive oil and place the dough ball in it. Cover the bowl with plastic wrap and let it rest in a warm place until the dough has doubled in size, about 1 hour and 30 minutes.
5. Generously flour a work surface and turn the dough out onto it, then cut it in half. Cover the dough with a clean kitchen towel and let rest for 15 minutes. Roll each piece of dough into a log, about 30 inches (75 cm) long and 2 inches (5 cm) thick. Loosely intertwine the logs and shape them into a ring, then press the ends together firmly.

CONTINUED ON PAGE 53

CONTINUED FROM PAGE 51

6 **To make the topping:** Gently position the 4 dyed eggs in the folds of the Easter bread, making sure they are spread out equally and secured in the dough folds. Place the bread on the prepared baking sheet. Cover with a clean kitchen towel and let rise for 45 minutes. After 30 minutes, preheat the oven to 350°F (180°C).

7 Just before baking, brush the top of bread with the beaten egg yolks. Do not brush the dyed eggs. Bake until the bread is golden brown, 20 to 25 minutes. Let cool completely on a wire rack before glazing.

8 In a small bowl, whisk together the confectioners' sugar, milk, and anise extract. (You can make your glaze as thin or as thick as you like; for a thicker glaze, add more confectioners' sugar, and for a thinner glaze, add more milk.) Spoon the glaze over the Easter bread. Decorate with rainbow nonpareils. Let dry on a wire rack.

Nonna Liliana Barone's

CASSATA CASALINGA

HOUSEWIVES' CASSATA CAKE

Prep time: 9 hours
Cook time: 40 minutes
Yield: One 12-inch (30 cm) cake

A *cassata* cake is synonymous with Sicily. In this slightly simplified version, delicate layers of Italian sponge cake are soaked in rum, topped with decadent ricotta frosting, and decorated with colorful candied fruits, providing a feast of textures and colors for the senses. Usually, a decorative layer of marzipan is placed around the cake, but Nonna Lilliana prefers to leave it out, cutting down on the sweetness and the time it takes to make.

RICOTTA FILLING

2½ pounds (1.1 kg) ricotta impastata

1¼ cups (250 g) granulated sugar

1 teaspoon vanilla extract

½ cup (90 g) mini semisweet chocolate chips

2½ ounces (70 g) zuccata (candied pumpkin) or candied orange peel, lemon peel, or citron, cut into ¼-inch (6 mm) dice

RICOTTA FROSTING

16 ounces (455 g) ricotta impastata

¼ cup (50 g) granulated sugar

SPONGE CAKE

Unsalted butter, for greasing

1½ cups (173 g) self-rising flour, plus more for dusting the pan

Confectioners' sugar, for dusting the pan

8 large eggs, separated

1 teaspoon vanilla extract

1 cup (200 g) granulated sugar

1. **To make the ricotta filling:** In a large bowl, stir together the ricotta, granulated sugar, and vanilla. Fold in the chocolate chips and zuccata and mix until fully incorporated. Cover the bowl with plastic wrap and refrigerate for at least 4 hours or up to overnight.
2. **To make the ricotta frosting:** In a medium bowl, stir together the ricotta and granulated sugar until smooth. Cover the bowl with plastic wrap and refrigerate for at least 4 hours or up to overnight.
3. **To make the sponge cake:** Preheat the oven to 375°F (190°C). Grease a 10-inch (25 cm) springform pan with butter and dust it with flour and a sprinkle of confectioners' sugar.
4. In a large bowl, using a handheld electric mixer, beat the egg whites at high speed until soft peaks form.
5. In another large bowl, with clean beaters, beat the vanilla, granulated sugar, and egg yolks at high speed until pale yellow, about 5 minutes. Add the egg whites to the yolk mixture. Mix at medium speed to incorporate. Add the flour, a little at a time, mixing at medium speed until fully incorporated. Transfer the batter to the prepared pan. Bake until the top of the cake is golden brown and springy, about 40 minutes. Let cool to room temperature.
6. **To make the soak:** In a small bowl, combine the rum and water.
7. **To assemble:** Line the bottom of a 10-inch (25 cm) springform pan with plastic wrap. Dust the sides of the pan with flour.

CONTINUED ON PAGE 56

CONTINUED FROM PAGE 54

SOAK

¼ cup (60 ml) white rum

¼ cup (60 ml) warm water

DECORATION

Candied fruits and nuts, such as orange peels, cherries, citron, and pistachios

8 Slice off the very top of the sponge cake dome and discard. Cut the cake horizontally into 3 even layers about 1 inch (2.5 cm) thick. Set aside the top layer of the cake.

9 Cut the 2 remaining layers into strips about 2½ inches (6 cm) wide; the strips should be the same width as the height of the springform pan. Reserve the rounded edges for the bottom layer of the cake. Trim the crust from the edges of the cake strips to make the edges straight.

10 Line the sides of the prepared pan with the cake strips. Line the bottom of the pan with the remaining pieces of cake with the rounded edges. Brush the cake with half of the soak. Add the ricotta filling and spread it evenly.

11 Trim the crust from the edges of the remaining cake layer, place it on top of the filling, and brush it with the remaining soak. Cover the cake with plastic wrap and refrigerate for at least 4 hours or overnight. Release the springform pan and invert the cake onto a serving platter. Spread the ricotta frosting over the cake and decorate it with candied fruits and nuts as desired. Serve chilled.

Nonna Carmela Tornatore's

SCIAUNI

RICOTTA-FILLED SICILIAN PASTRIES

Prep time: 45 minutes

Cook time: 15 minutes

Yield: About 17 pastries

DOUGH

1 cup (240 ml) white wine, such as Chablis

3 cups (360 g) all-purpose or 00 flour, plus more for dusting

½ cup (100 g) shortening

FILLING

16 ounces (455 g) ricotta impastata

¼ cup (50 g) sugar

¾ teaspoon ground cinnamon

6 tablespoons mini semisweet chocolate chips

ASSEMBLY

1 large egg white

Oil, for frying (use any oil you like)

Sugar, for sprinkling

Sciauni are sweet, fried calzones, typical of eastern Sicily. Every year, Nonna Carmela and her daughter fill them with a sheep's milk ricotta mixed with a little sugar, cinnamon, and a few semisweet chocolate chips to keep the flavors of Sicily alive in their home.

1. **To make the dough:** In a small bowl, whisk together the wine and ¼ cup (60 ml) of water.
2. In a medium bowl, add the flour and shortening. With a pastry cutter or a fork, cut the shortening into the flour. Add the wine-water mixture, mixing with a fork until absorbed.
3. Flour a work surface and turn the dough out onto it. Knead the dough with your hands until smooth and elastic. The dough should be humid to the touch but not sticky. Cover with a clean kitchen towel and let rest for 10 minutes.
4. **To make the filling:** In a medium bowl, stir together the ricotta, sugar, and cinnamon. Fold in the chocolate chips.
5. **To assemble:** Divide the dough into 4 pieces. Using a rolling pin, roll out 1 piece of dough at a time, ⅛ inch (3 mm) thick. Using a 5-inch (13 cm) round cookie cutter, cut out circles of dough. Reroll and cut any scraps.
6. In a small bowl, beat the egg white and 1 tablespoon of water.
7. Place about 2 tablespoons (30 g) of filling in the center of each circle. Brush the dough edges with the egg wash and fold the dough over. With your fingers, firmly press together the dough surrounding the filling and seal the edges with the tines of a fork. Trim any edges with a ravioli cutter, if you like.
8. Heat about 2½ inches (6 cm) of oil in a small stockpot over high heat. Working in batches, fry the pastries until golden brown, 2 to 3 minutes per batch. With a slotted spoon, transfer to a serving dish and immediately sprinkle with sugar. Serve at room temperature.

Nonna Gilda Castiello Taormina's

PASTIERA NAPOLETANA

WHEAT PIE

Prep time: 1 hour

Cook time: 1 hour 55 minutes

Yield: 8 to 10 servings

Nonna Gilda makes these classic grain pies two at a time for the Easter holidays. An old Neapolitan tradition mandates that the *pastiera* be made a few days before the Easter holidays—but no later than the Thursday or Good Friday of Holy Week—so that all the flavors have a chance to meld.

CRUST

2½ cups (300 g) all-purpose or 00 flour, plus more for dusting

½ cup (100 g) sugar

3 large eggs

2½ tablespoons vegetable shortening, plus more for greasing

Dash salt

Zest of 1 lemon

FILLING

2 ounces (55 g) spelt (hulled wheat)

2 cups (480 ml) cold water

2 large eggs, separated

12 ounces (340 g) whole milk ricotta

1 cup (200 g) sugar

2 teaspoons vanilla extract

½ teaspoon orange extract

¼ cup (36 g) citron or candied fruit (optional)

1. **To make the crust:** In a large mixing bowl, combine the flour, sugar, eggs, shortening, salt, and lemon zest. Mix with your hands until a firm dough forms. Flatten the dough into a disk, wrap it in plastic wrap, and refrigerate for at least 1 hour or up to overnight.
2. **To make the filling:** Rinse the spelt under cold water. To a small saucepan, add the water and the rinsed wheat; cook until tender, stirring occasionally with a wooden spoon, 30 to 40 minutes. Drain and set aside until cool.
3. In the bowl of a stand mixer fitted with the paddle attachment, beat the egg yolks at medium speed until fluffy and lemon colored, about 5 minutes. Add the ricotta, wheat, and sugar, and mix until combined. Add the vanilla extract, orange extract, and citron (if using) and mix until incorporated.
4. In a medium bowl, beat the egg whites with a handheld electric mixer until soft peaks form. Gently fold the egg whites into the ricotta mixture. Set aside.
5. **To assemble:** Preheat the oven to 350°F (175°C). Grease a 9-inch (23 cm) round pie pan with vegetable shortening.
6. On a lightly floured surface, using a rolling pin, roll out the dough into a 12-inch (30 cm) circle, about ½ inch (6 mm) thick. Roll the dough up onto the rolling pin and unfurl it over the pie pan, allowing the excess to hang off the sides. Add the filling and trim the excess dough. On a lightly floured surface, roll out the excess dough into a ⅛-inch-thick (3 mm) circle. With a ravioli cutter, cut out 1-inch (2.5 cm) strips and place them in a lattice pattern over the filling, pressing the edges slightly to adhere. Trim any excess dough.
7. Bake until the crust has colored and the filling has set, about 1 hour and 15 minutes. Let cool before serving.

Nonna Romana Sciddurlo's

PESCHE CON ALKERMES

ITALIAN PEACH PASTRIES

Prep time: 30 minutes
Cook time: 28 minutes
Yield: 6 pastries

If you peer into the windows of many bakeries in Italy, you will see these gorgeous peaches staring back at you. Italian-Americans have taken to naming them peach cookies, and while some of them are indeed cookies, here, they are little half spheres of cake with velvety Pastry Cream (page 6) sandwiched between them. These peaches are soaked in a sweet, bitter, red liqueur called Alkermes, which is used in many desserts. A final coating of granulated sugar gives them the look of real peaches, making them perfect for a spring holiday such as Easter.

CAKE

Nonstick cooking spray, for greasing
2 cups (240 g) all-purpose or 00 flour
1½ teaspoons baking powder
5 large eggs, at room temperature
1 cup (200 g) sugar

ASSEMBLY

1 cup (240 ml) Alkermes liqueur (or Aperol or grenadine)
Sugar, for rolling the pastries
1 Pastry Cream recipe (page 6)
Fresh mint leaves, for decorating

1. **To make the cakes:** Preheat the oven to 350°F (180°C). Grease two oven-safe 6-cavity silicone half-sphere molds with cooking spray. In a small bowl, whisk together the flour and baking powder.
2. In the bowl of a stand mixer fitted with the paddle attachment, mix the eggs and sugar at medium speed for 30 seconds. Increase the speed to high and mix until the mixture is pale yellow, doubles in volume, and ribbons form, 15 to 20 minutes. Reduce the speed to low. Spoon in the dry ingredients, a little at a time, mixing until fully absorbed.
3. Fill each cavity of the prepared molds with ¼ cup (60 ml) of the batter and place the molds on a baking sheet. Bake until the cakes are golden and springy in the middle, about 20 minutes. Cool to room temperature.
4. **To assemble:** Pour the Alkermes into a small bowl. Put some sugar into a shallow dish. Have some jumbo paper cupcakes liners handy.
5. Using a very sharp knife, slice the domes off the tops of the cakes so they have a straight edge. Either with a knife or your fingers, slightly hollow out each cake, removing about 1 tablespoon of cake crumb from the center. Place about 3 tablespoons of pastry cream in the hollow of each cake. Place another half of cake over the cream to form a sphere. Some cream should peek out of the edges; smooth the cream with a knife so it's flush with the cake.
6. Dip the spheres into the Alkermes, just until the sponge is completely colored. Do not immerse for too long. Roll the spheres in the sugar, making sure they're completely coated. Place each pastry into a jumbo paper cupcake liner. Decorate with fresh mint leaves.

Nonna Romana Sciddurlo's

SCARCELLA DI PASQUA

PUGLIESE EASTER BREAD

Prep time: 20 minutes
Cook time: 20 minutes
Yield: 5 braided scarcelle

Nonna Romana's classic Easter bread from Puglia is my absolute favorite thing about Easter. A classic Pugliese *scarcella*, or *gurrugulo*, as it is called in Nonna's hometown of Mola di Bari, is traditionally given to children for Easter. Usually it is shaped into a braided ring and an egg is placed on top with a cross over it to symbolize fertility. The olive oil-based dough is super easy to work with and is more like a cookie than bread after it's baked, and it has the most wonderful lemon scent.

DOUGH

4¼ cups (510 g) all-purpose or 00 flour, plus more for working the dough

2 teaspoons baking powder

4 large eggs

1 cup (200 g) sugar

¾ cup (180 ml) olive oil

Zest of 1 lemon or 1 tablespoon Nonna Laura's Sweet Lemon Zest (page 8)

DECORATION

5 large eggs, dyed (not hard-boiled eggs)

1 large egg, beaten

Rainbow nonpareils, for decorating

1. **To make the dough:** Preheat the oven to 400°F (200°C). Line two baking sheets with parchment paper.
2. In a large bowl, whisk together the flour and baking powder. Set aside.
3. In the bowl of a stand mixer fitted with the paddle attachment, add the eggs, sugar, olive oil, and lemon zest; mix at medium speed until combined. Add the flour-baking powder mixture and mix at medium speed until absorbed.
4. Generously flour a work surface and turn the dough out onto it. Flour your hands. To make the braids, divide the dough into 15 equal pieces, reserving enough dough to secure the eggs in step 7. With your floured hands, roll one piece of dough into a rope about 14 inches (35 cm) long and ¾ inch (2 cm) thick. Repeat with 2 more pieces of dough. Pinch the 3 ropes together at one end. Slowly and carefully, braid them to the very end and pinch the end of the braid closed; trim any uneveness with a knife. Bring the ends of the braid together, overlapping them slightly, to form a ring, then transfer to a prepared baking sheet. Repeat with the remaining pieces of dough until you have 5 rings total.
5. **To decorate:** For each ring, press the dough together where the ends overlap and place 1 egg on top of the seam.
6. Divide the reserved dough into 10 pieces. Roll each piece into a small rope about ¼ inch (6 mm) thick. Place 2 strips over each egg, forming a cross, pressing each end into the braid to secure it. Gently press the dough together where it overlaps on top of the egg.
7. Brush all the dough with the beaten egg, being careful not to get any on the eggshells. Sprinkle with nonpareils and bake until the tops of the braids are lightly golden and shiny and the bottoms are nicely browned, 15 to 18 minutes. Serve at room temperature.

Nonna Romana Sciddurlo's

ANGINETTI

LEMON DROP COOKIES

Prep time: 15 minutes

Cook time: 15 minutes

Yield: About 30 cookies

These lovely lemon drops are made in honor of many occasions in southern Italian families. Nonna Romana always makes these delightful cookies, in a variety of shapes, around Easter because their vibrant lemon flavor pairs perfectly with the onset of spring.

COOKIES

3 cups (360 g) all-purpose or 00 flour, plus more for dusting

2 teaspoons baking powder

Pinch salt

¾ cup (150 g) granulated sugar

½ cup (1 stick/120 g) butter, at room temperature

Zest of 2 lemons or 2 tablespoons Nonna Laura's Sweet Lemon Zest (page 8)

1½ teaspoons lemon extract

1 packet (½ ounce/15 g) Italian vanilla powder or 1 teaspoon vanilla extract

2 large eggs, at room temperature

2 tablespoons heavy whipping cream, at room temperature

GLAZE

1 cup (120 g) confectioners' sugar

Zest of 1 lemon

Juice of 1 lemon or 1 tablespoon Nonna Laura's Sweet Lemon Zest (page 8)

1 teaspoon vanilla extract

3 tablespoons whole milk

White nonpareils, for decorating

1. **To make the cookies:** Preheat the oven to 350°F (180°C). Line 2 baking sheets with parchment paper.
2. In a medium bowl, whisk together the flour, baking powder, and salt.
3. In the bowl of a stand mixer fitted with the paddle attachment, add the sugar, butter, lemon zest, lemon extract, and vanilla. Mix at medium speed until fluffy, about 5 minutes. With the mixer at medium speed, add the eggs, one at a time, mixing until fully incorporated before adding the next. Reduce the speed to low and add the flour mixture; mix until almost fully absorbed. Add the heavy cream and mix until just combined.
4. Lightly flour a work surface and turn the dough out onto it. Cut the dough in half. With one half of the dough, make twists: Flour your hands and roll it into a ½-inch-thick (13 mm) rope. Cut the rope into pieces, about 8 inches (20 cm) long. Fold each piece in half, twist it 3 times, and press the ends together. With the other half of the dough, make knots: Flour your hands. Grab a chunk of dough and roll it into a rope about 6 inches (15 cm) long and ¾ inch (2 cm) thick. Shape the rope into a knot by bringing one end over the other, then through the middle. Repeat with the remaining dough.
5. Arrange the cookies on the prepared baking sheets, 2 inches (5 cm) apart. Bake until the bottoms are golden brown, 12 to 15 minutes. Let cool completely before icing.
6. **To make the glaze:** In a small bowl, whisk together the confectioners' sugar, lemon zest, lemon juice, vanilla, and milk. Dip the cookies into the glaze, sprinkle with the nonpareils, and place them on a wire rack to dry.

Nonna Vivian Cardia's

FOCACCIA GENOVESE CON CIPOLLE

GENOVESE-STYLE FOCACCIA WITH ONIONS

Prep time: 2 hours
Cook time: 30 minutes
Yield: 8 to 10 servings

If you've ever had a piece of warm, freshly baked *focaccia* in Italy, you'll understand why it's such an important part of Italian cuisine. Romans would give pieces of focaccia as an offering to their gods, and ever since, every region has its own specialty focaccia. This version is topped simply with white onions. What sets it apart is the water and oil emulsion that fills tiny indentations made by hand in the dough.

DOUGH

½ cup (120 ml) extra-virgin olive oil, divided, plus more for brushing

2 packets (¼ ounce/7 g each) active dry yeast

1½ cups (360 ml) warm water

4 cups (480 g) all-purpose or 00 flour

2 teaspoons salt

FOCACCIA

6 tablespoons extra-virgin olive oil, divided

1½ teaspoons coarse salt

2 large onions, halved, with halves sliced into thin half-moons

1. **To make the dough:** In the bowl of a stand mixer fitted with the dough hook attachment, combine ¼ cup (60 ml) of the olive oil, the yeast, and warm water. Let stand until the yeast dissolves, 5 to 8 minutes.
2. In a medium bowl, whisk together the flour and salt. With the mixer running at low speed, gradually add the flour. Mix until a smooth, supple dough forms, 8 to 10 minutes.
3. Brush a large bowl with olive oil and transfer the dough to it. Brush the dough ball with olive oil too. Cover the bowl with plastic wrap and set aside in a warm place until the dough doubles in size, about 1 hour. Punch down the dough.
4. Preheat the oven to 475°F (240°C).
5. Add the remaining ¼ cup (60 ml) olive oil to a 13 by 18-inch (33 by 46 cm) baking sheet and spread it evenly, making sure to coat the bottom and sides of the pan. With your fingers, spread the dough to the edges of the pan, starting from the center and working outward. Cover the dough with plastic wrap and set aside in a warm place for 1 hour. Remove the plastic wrap, and using your fingertips, lightly make indentations all over the dough.
6. **To assemble the focaccia:** In a small bowl, whisk together ¼ cup (60 ml) of the olive oil with ¼ cup (60 ml) of water. Pour the mixture over the dough, making sure to fill all the indentations. Sprinkle the dough with the salt.
7. In a medium bowl, drizzle the onions with the remaining 2 tablespoons olive oil. Toss to coat. Scatter the onions over the focaccia. Bake until the top of the focaccia is golden and the onions have completely softened, about 30 minutes.

Nonna Romana Sciddurlo's

FRITTATA DI CIME DI RAPA E SALSICCIA

BROCCOLI RABE AND SAUSAGE FRITTATA

Prep time: 10 minutes
Cook time: 55 minutes
Yield: 6 to 8 servings

Nonna Romana likes to recall when she and her seven brothers and sisters would go into *la campagna* (the countryside) of Mola di Bari to celebrate *la Pasquetta*. Such an occasion would require a frittata fit for an army! Today, our family celebrates *la Pasquetta* in Nonna's Brooklyn basement apartment, but this frittata, which is baked instead of fried, keeps filling our stomachs and our souls, year after year.

- 1 teaspoon salt, plus more for boiling
- ½ pound (225 g) broccoli rabe, washed, ends trimmed, and chopped into bite-size pieces
- ½ cup (120 ml) plus 3 tablespoons extra-virgin olive oil, divided
- ½ pound (225 g) sweet Italian sausage, casings removed
- 8 large eggs
- 3 cloves garlic, minced
- ¾ cup (90 g) plain bread crumbs
- ¼ cup (60 ml) whole milk
- 1½ cups (150 g) grated Pecorino Romano cheese
- ¼ teaspoon black pepper

1. Bring a medium pot of lightly salted water to a boil. Drop in the broccoli rabe and cook just until the stems are tender, about 5 minutes. Drain and run under cold water. Squeeze out the excess moisture with your hands. Set aside.
2. In a medium cast-iron skillet (see Nonna Romana Says), heat 1 tablespoon of the olive oil over medium-high heat. Add the sausage and cook, breaking it up with a wooden spoon, until nicely browned, 7 to 9 minutes. Transfer to a plate and set aside.
3. In a medium bowl, whisk together the eggs, garlic, bread crumbs, milk, cheese, 1 teaspoon salt, pepper, and 2 tablespoons of the olive oil. Mix in the broccoli rabe and sausage.
4. Preheat the oven to 400°F (200°C).
5. In a medium cast-iron or oven-safe skillet, heat the remaining ½ cup (120 ml) olive oil over high heat. Add the egg mixture and spread it evenly in the pan using a spoon or a rubber spatula. Cook until the eggs have just set around the edges, 2 to 3 minutes. Transfer the skillet to the middle rack of the oven and bake until the middle of the frittata is set and golden brown 30 to 35 minutes. Serve warm or at room temperature.

Nonna Romana Says

This frittata is ideally made in a cast-iron skillet, but if you must use another pan, make sure to add a bit more olive oil to the bottom.

Nonna Romana Sciddurlo's

CAVOLFIORI E CARCIOFINI FRITTI IN PASTELLA

BATTERED CAULIFLOWER AND BABY ARTICHOKES

Prep time: 10 minutes

Cook time: 25 minutes

Yield: 8 to 10 servings

Nonna Romana's classic Puglia-style batter, bursting with garlic, cheese, and mint, creates a light, crispy coating on your favorite vegetables. Artichokes and cauliflower are a wonderful pairing of flavors and have contrasting textures that pack a ton of flavor in every bite.

2 lemons, halved

2 pounds (910 g) fresh baby artichokes

1¼ cups (125 g) grated Parmigiano-Reggiano cheese

½ cup (32 g) minced fresh mint

6 cloves garlic, minced

1 teaspoon salt

2 large eggs, beaten

10 ounces (280 g) fresh cauliflower florets

Oil, for frying

1. Fill a large bowl with cold water and add the lemons.
2. Clean the artichokes by removing the outer leaves until you reach the yellow or light green parts. Remove and discard the stems. Quarter the artichokes vertically through the stems and place them in the prepared bowl.
3. In another large bowl, add the cheese, mint, garlic, salt, eggs, and 1½ cups plus 2 tablespoons (380 ml) of water. Whisk until a smooth batter forms.
4. Pat the artichokes dry with a paper towel and add them to the batter, then add the cauliflower florets and mix until everything is evenly coated.
5. Line a plate with paper towels. In a large heavy-bottomed skillet, heat about 1½ inches (4 cm) of oil over medium-high heat. Working in batches, fry the battered vegetables until golden brown, 5 to 6 minutes per batch. Transfer to the paper towel-lined plate. Serve hot.

Nonna Romana Sciddurlo's

CARCIOFI RIPIENI ALLA PUGLIESE

PUGLIA-STYLE STUFFED ARTICHOKES

Prep time: 15 minutes
Cook time: 30 minutes
Yield: 4 servings

Nonna Romana's stuffed-artichoke recipe from Mola di Bari has been made in my family for generations. The beautiful spring peas and savory pancetta cook up some serious flavor and make for a vibrant side dish. Traditionally, these would be made for Easter, and any leftovers would have been taken into the country to celebrate *la Pasquetta* picnic.

- 2 lemons, halved
- 4 medium fresh artichokes
- 1 cup (100 g) grated Pecorino Romano cheese
- ½ cup (60 g) plain bread crumbs
- 2 large eggs
- 3 cloves garlic, minced
- 1 tablespoon minced fresh parsley
- ½ teaspoon salt, plus more to taste
- ¼ teaspoon black pepper, plus more to taste
- 6 tablespoons extra-virgin olive oil, divided
- 2 tablespoons whole milk, as needed
- 12 ounces (340 g) frozen peas, thawed
- 1 medium onion, cut into ¼-inch (6 mm) dice
- 4 ounces (113 g) pancetta, cut into ½-inch (13 mm) cubes

1. Fill a large bowl with cold water and add the lemons.
2. Clean the artichokes by removing the outer leaves until you reach the light green part. Remove and discard the tough outer skin from the stems. Trim about ¾ inch (2 cm) from the leaves, and about ¼ inch (6 mm) from the stems. Peel the stems. Halve the artichokes vertically through the stems. With a small spoon, scoop out and discard the fuzzy choke. Place the artichoke halves in the prepared bowl.
3. In another large bowl, stir together the cheese, bread crumbs, eggs, garlic, parsley, salt, pepper, and 3 tablespoons (45 ml) of the olive oil. If the mixture is dry, add 1 tablespoon of milk at a time until you achieve a soft consistency. The mixture should be soft, not runny.
4. Preheat the oven to 350°F (180°C).
5. In the bottom of a 9 by 13-inch (23 by 33 cm) stovetop-safe baking dish, add the peas, onion, pancetta, and the remaining 3 tablespoons olive oil. Season with salt and pepper. Mix until everything is evenly coated.
6. Spread 2 tablespoons of the cheese-bread crumb mixture over each artichoke half. Place the stuffed artichoke, filled side up, over the bed of peas. Add 2 cups (480 ml) of water to the baking dish and bring it to a boil over high heat, then transfer the pan to the oven and bake until the peas are cooked and the artichokes are tender, about 30 minutes.

Nonna Romana Says

I usually like to make these the night before I serve them, so the filling has a chance to rest and absorb all the flavors.

Nonna Lorella Colandrea's

FRITTATA DI SPAGHETTI ALLA NAPOLETANA

NEAPOLITAN SPAGHETTI PIE

Prep time: 10 minutes
Cook time: 20 minutes
Yield: 6 to 8 servings

This traditional spaghetti pie is a post-Easter favorite at Nonna Lorella's house. It's the perfect thing to make if you're going on a picnic, because it tastes divine at room temperature, and it can easily be served by cutting it into wedges. It's also a great way to utilize any leftover pasta you have, even if it has sauce on it. The secret to flipping it without making a mess is not to rush and to let the bottom cook enough to get the pasta nice and brown. "You want to make sure you have crispy edges all over," says Nonna Lorella. I totally agree—that's the best part!

1 cup (250 g) whole-milk ricotta

5 ounces (142 g) dried sausage, cut into ¼-inch (6 mm) dice (you can also use prosciutto, pancetta, or ham)

5 large eggs, beaten

¾ cup (75 g) grated Pecorino Romano cheese

4 ounces (113 g) fresh mozzarella cheese, shredded

1 teaspoon salt

½ teaspoon black pepper

1 tablespoon unsalted butter, at room temperature

8 ounces (225 g) dried spaghetti, cooked al dente (you can also use leftover spaghetti, even if it has sauce on it)

2 tablespoons extra-virgin olive oil

1. In a large bowl, whisk together the ricotta, sausage, eggs, Pecorino Romano, mozzarella, salt, pepper, and butter. Add the spaghetti and mix until evenly coated.
2. In a large nonstick skillet, heat the oil over medium-high heat. Add the pasta mixture and spread it into an even layer. Reduce the heat to medium-low. Cover the skillet and cook until the bottom and sides are set, 10 to 12 minutes.
3. Wearing oven mitts on both hands, uncover the skillet and place a large plate or large, flat lid over the pan. Quickly flip the pan over so the spaghetti pie rests on the plate. Quickly slide it back into the skillet and cook until set, 5 to 7 minutes.

THANKSGIVING

Nonna Maria Pesce's

LASAGNE DI ZUCCA

BUTTERNUT SQUASH LASAGNA

Prep time: 35 minutes

Cook time: 1 hour 40 minutes

Yield: 6 servings

SAUCE

2 tablespoons extra-virgin olive oil

3 ribs celery, cut into ¼-inch (6 mm) dice

1 small carrot, cut into ¼-inch (6 mm) dice

1 small onion, cut into ¼-inch (6 mm) dice

¾ cup (182 g) canned crushed tomatoes

¼ cup (60 ml) cold water

1 teaspoon salt, plus more to taste

Black pepper

2½ pounds (1.2 kg) butternut squash, cut into 1-inch (2.5 cm) dice

LASAGNA

Unsalted butter, for greasing

Salt

17 or 18 dried lasagna pasta noodles

2 large eggs, beaten

16 ounces (455 g) fresh mozzarella cheese, cut into ¼-inch (6 mm) cubes

12 ounces (340 g) mortadella or ham, about 12 slices (optional)

½ cup (50 g) grated Parmigiano-Reggiano cheese, divided

Italian-Americans can't seem to celebrate Thanksgiving without a pasta course preceding the turkey. You know, just in case a twelve-pound (5.4 kg) turkey with all the trimmings isn't enough food. I first tasted Nonna Maria's yummy, autumn-inspired lasagna three years ago when my boyfriend Nick invited me over for our first Thanksgiving together. When I told her it was fantastic, I'm sure she thought that I was just being polite (after all, I was her son's new girlfriend and she is a quintessential Italian Mamma), but my reaction was totally genuine. She starts by cooking chunks of butternut squash with aromatics and purees it into a velvety sauce, which adds a delightful sweetness to the dish. She then layers it with delicious mortadella and bakes it to perfection. It even tastes great the next day, reheated after a marathon of Black Friday shopping.

1. **To make the sauce:** In a large skillet, heat the oil over medium heat and add the celery, carrot, and onion. Cook, stirring occasionally, until soft, 7 to 10 minutes. Stir in the tomatoes, cold water, 1 teaspoon salt, and pepper to taste. Cook for 15 minutes.
2. In a large saucepan over high heat, bring 4 cups (960 ml) of water to a boil. Stir in the butternut squash and season with salt to taste. Cook until soft, 25 to 30 minutes. Remove from the heat, drain, and let cool for 15 minutes.
3. Transfer the cooled butternut squash to a blender with the vegetable mixture and puree until smooth. Transfer the sauce to a medium bowl.
4. **To make the lasagna:** Preheat the oven to 400°F (200°C). Butter a 9 by 13-inch (23 by 33 cm) baking pan.
5. Bring a medium pot of salted water to a boil. Drop in the lasagna noodles and cook until very al dente, about 10 minutes. Drain and rinse the noodles under cold running water. Fold all the noodles over the edge of the pot to dry.

CONTINUED ON PAGE 76

CONTINUED FROM PAGE 75

6 To the prepared baking dish, add 1¼ cups (300 ml) of sauce and spread it into an even layer and cover it with about 4 lasagna noodles. Spread another ½ cup (120 ml) of sauce over the noodles and drizzle with 2 to 3 teaspoons of the beaten egg. Top with one-quarter of the mozzarella, one-third of the mortadella (if using), and 2 tablespoons of the Parmigiano-Reggiano. Repeat the layering twice more. Add the final layer of noodles to cover the entire surface. Spread 1 cup (240 ml) of the sauce over the noodles and top with the remaining beaten egg, the remaining mozzarella, and the remaining 2 tablespoons Parmigiano-Reggiano.

7 Bake until the pasta is very easily pierced with a fork, 30 to 40 minutes. Let rest for 15 to 20 minutes before cutting and serving with any leftover sauce on the side.

Nonna Liliana Barone's

RIPIENO DI RISO E CARNE

RICE AND MEAT STUFFING

Prep time: 15 minutes
Cook time: 1 hour 15 minutes
Yield: 8 to 10 servings

The concept of stuffing has always been a bit strange for Italian-Americans to grasp, especially for the immigrant generation. So, when Nonna Liliana was coming up with a way to make stuffing, she immediately thought about the foods Italians *do* stuff: peppers, eggplant, etc. This stuffing is full of Italian flavors and is reminiscent of classic stuffed peppers; at the same time, it is satisfying and goes well with classic American roasted turkey.

½ teaspoon salt, plus a pinch and more to taste

1 cup (185 g) long-grain rice, rinsed

2 ribs celery, minced

1 small carrot, minced

1 pound (455 g) sweet Italian sausage, casings removed

1 pound (455 g) ground beef

2 bay leaves

5 tablespoons extra-virgin olive oil

6 bunches scallions, green stalks removed and white bulbs cut into ¼-inch (6 mm) dice

Black pepper

¼ cup (34 g) pignoli (pine nuts)

10 ounces (280 g) cremini mushrooms, sliced

1½ teaspoons fennel seeds

1 cup (240 ml) beef broth

1. In a large saucepan over high heat, bring 3½ cups (840 ml) of water and ½ teaspoon salt to a boil. Add the rice and boil, uncovered, until the rice is halfway cooked, about 15 minutes. Drain and spread the rice in a thin layer on a large plate to cool.
2. In a small saucepan, add the celery and carrot and enough water to cover. Bring to a boil over high heat and cook, uncovered, for 5 minutes. Drain and set aside.
3. Heat a large skillet over medium-high heat and add the sausage, ground beef, a pinch of salt, and the bay leaves. Cook, stirring occasionally, until the meat is nicely browned, 7 to 10 minutes. Drain the fat and set aside.
4. In large heavy-bottomed skillet, heat the olive oil over medium heat. Add the scallions and season with salt and pepper. Cook, stirring occasionally, until the scallions are soft, 10 to 12 minutes. Add the pignoli and cook, stirring occasionally, for 2 to 3 minutes. Add the mushrooms and cook, stirring occasionally, for 4 to 6 minutes. Add the meat mixture, the fennel seeds, and the carrot-celery mixture. Cook, stirring occasionally, for 2 to 3 minutes. Stir in the broth and the cooled rice. Cook until the rice is tender, about 5 minutes. Transfer to a serving dish. Serve warm.

Nonna Rosa Carmelo's

VERDURE AL FORNO CON PARMIGIANO

PARMIGIANO–ROASTED VEGETABLES

Prep time: 10 minutes
Cook time: 35 minutes
Yield: 6 to 8 servings

Nonna and I love this easy vegetable dish because it's a breeze to prep. Toss everything in the bread crumb and cheese mixture and roast until the veggies are beautifully charred. Feel free to swap out the veggies for your seasonal favorites.

10 cloves garlic

1 pound (455 g) small red potatoes, quartered

9 ounces (255 g) Brussels sprouts, ends trimmed, halved

8 ounces (225 g) baby carrots

1 large sweet potato, peeled and cut into 1½-inch (4 cm) chunks

¾ cup (180 ml) extra-virgin olive oil

½ cup (50 g) grated Parmigiano-Reggiano cheese

¼ cup (30 g) plain bread crumbs

1½ teaspoons salt

½ teaspoon black pepper

5 fresh rosemary sprigs

5 fresh thyme sprigs

1. Preheat the oven to 450°F (230°C).
2. On a baking sheet, spread the vegetables into an even layer. Drizzle the olive oil over the vegetables and top with the cheese, bread crumbs, salt, pepper, the rosemary, and thyme; using your hands or a large spoon, toss or stir the vegetables until evenly coated.
3. Roast for 30 to 35 minutes, turning the vegetables halfway through the cooking time. Serve immediately.

Nonna Maria Pesce's

TACCHINO AGLI AGRUMI

THANKSGIVING CITRUS TURKEY

Prep time: 15 minutes
Cook time: 3 hour 10 minutes
Yield: 8 to 10 servings

No Thanksgiving holiday would be complete without a turkey. Nonna Maria confesses that she was a bit lost her first Thanksgiving in America when faced with the unfamiliar bird. (In Italy, turkey is rarely eaten; capon, if anything, is prepared in its place.) But over the years she learned to love the American tradition. She did add her own Italian flair to the preparation, of course!

TURKEY

13-pound (5.9 kg) turkey, thawed if frozen

½ cup (1 stick/120 g) salted butter, at room temperature

⅓ cup (75 ml) extra-virgin olive oil

¼ cup (8 g) minced fresh rosemary

Salt and black pepper

1 navel orange, halved

1 lemon, halved

1 apple, halved

5 cloves garlic

4 to 5 fresh rosemary sprigs

4 to 5 fresh thyme sprigs

6 to 7 fresh sage leaves

2 tablespoons dry white wine, such as Pinot Grigio

TRIMMINGS

3 lemons, halved

1 orange, quartered

15 cloves garlic

1 cup (240 ml) dry white wine, such as Pinot Grigio

1. **To make the turkey:** Preheat the oven to 350°F (180°C).
2. Remove the neck and giblets from the turkey's cavity and discard. Using kitchen shears or a sharp knife, trim the skin from the neck of the turkey and discard. Pat the turkey dry, inside and out, with paper towels. Slide your hand under the skin of a breast, separating it from the meat. Repeat with the other breast. With your hands, place the butter under the loosened skin and spread it evenly on both sides of the breast.
3. In a small bowl, stir together the olive oil and rosemary. Rub the mixture over the entire surface of the turkey. Season well with salt and pepper all over and inside the cavity.
4. Fill the cavity with the halved orange, lemon, apple, garlic, rosemary, thyme, sage, and pour in the wine.
5. **To trim the turkey:** Place the turkey, breast side up, inside the rack of a roasting pan. Place the halved lemons, orange quarters, and garlic around the turkey. Pour the wine and 1 cup (240 ml) of water into the bottom of the pan.
6. Tent the turkey with aluminum foil and roast for 2 hours and 30 minutes. Remove the foil and roast until an instant-read meat thermometer reads 175° to 180°F (79° to 82°C), 30 to 40 minutes. Let stand for 15 to 20 minutes before slicing and serving.

Nonna Maria Pesce's

FUNGHI E PISELLI CON MARSALA

MARSALA PEAS AND MUSHROOMS

Prep time: 5 minutes
Cook time: 30 minutes
Yield: 4 to 6 servings

It's amazing how just a splash of Marsala wine can add so much flavor to a dish. Nonna Maria loves dressing up simple peas and mushrooms, which soak up the wine beautifully, as an elegant holiday side dish that is anything but boring.

2 tablespoons extra-virgin olive oil

1 large onion, cut into ½-inch (13 mm) dice

Salt and black pepper

10 ounces (280 g) frozen peas, thawed

10 ounces (280 g) cremini mushrooms, sliced

¼ cup (60 ml) sweet Marsala wine

1. In a medium skillet, heat the olive oil over medium heat and add the onion. Season with salt and pepper as desired and cook, stirring occasionally, until the onion is very soft, 10 to 12 minutes.
2. Stir in the peas, mushrooms, and a bit more salt. Cook, stirring occasionally, until some water has been drawn out of the mushrooms, 5 to 7 minutes. Stir in the Marsala and 2 tablespoons of water. Cook until no alcohol can be tasted and the liquid has reduced by half, 7 to 10 minutes.

Nonna Antoinette Capodicci's

RISOTTO ALLA ZUCCA

PUMPKIN RISOTTO

Prep time: 10 minutes
Cook time: 30 minutes
Yield: 10 to 12 servings

This incredibly rich risotto will leave all your guests satisfied. It gets its lovely color from the pumpkin puree and its unique flavor from the Fontina cheese, which takes the place of butter in the *mantecare* process, when the ingredients are creamed together. This recipe makes a large batch that Nonna Antoinette usually serves buffet-style for her big Italian-American Thanksgiving, which never has fewer than a dozen people.

2 quarts (1.9 L) chicken broth

3 tablespoons extra-virgin olive oil

6 ounces (170 g) pancetta, cut into ¼-inch (6 mm) dice

1 large red onion, cut into ¼-inch (6 mm) dice

2 cloves garlic, minced

24 ounces (679 g) Arborio rice, rinsed

1 pound (455 g) butternut squash, fresh or frozen, cut into ½-inch (13 mm) dice

1 can (15 ounces/425 g) pure pumpkin (not pumpkin pie filling)

6 ounces (170 g) Parmigiano-Reggiano cheese, coarsely grated

6 ounces (170 g) Fontina cheese, cut into ½-inch (13 mm) dice

2 teaspoons salt

Black pepper

Dash ground nutmeg

1. In a small stockpot over medium-high heat, bring the chicken broth to a simmer. Reduce the heat to low and keep it at a simmer.
2. In a large heavy-bottomed skillet, heat the olive oil over medium heat and add the pancetta; cook, stirring occasionally, until crispy 5 to 7 minutes. Add the onion and garlic, and cook, stirring occasionally, until the garlic is golden, 2 to 3 minutes. Add the rice and stir until it's coated in oil and lightly toasted, 2 to 3 minutes. Add the butternut squash and cook, stirring occasionally, for 5 minutes.
3. Reduce the heat to low and stir in 1 cup (240 ml) of the simmering broth. When the broth has been absorbed, stir in another 1 cup (240 ml). Continue this process, stirring frequently to prevent sticking, until all the broth is absorbed and the rice is al dente, 20 to 25 minutes.
4. Add the pumpkin, Parmigiano-Reggiano, and Fontina; stir until the cheeses are melted and everything is fully incorporated. Taste and season with salt, pepper, and a dash of nutmeg. Let rest for 10 minutes before serving.

Nonna Romana Sciddurlo's

RIPIENO DI CIME DI RAPA E SALSICCIA

BROCCOLI RABE AND SAUSAGE STUFFING

Prep time: 15 minutes
Cook time: 1 hour 20 minutes
Yield: 8 servings

Growing up as a first-generation Italian-American, I would sometimes long for classic American fare in an attempt to assimilate with the kids at school. My brother and I would take trips to the supermarket in secret to buy boxed stuffing (don't judge), cook it while no one was in the kitchen, and pray no one else noticed it on the table. The secrecy eventually became too much, and I realized I needed to come up with a stuffing recipe the rest of my family would want to eat. Nonna Romana actually looks forward to this stuffing every year!

½ cup (1 stick/120 g) unsalted butter, melted, plus more for greasing

1 large loaf Italian bread, torn into bite-size pieces (about 8 cups/280 g)

¼ cup (60 ml) extra-virgin olive oil, divided

1 pound (455 g) sweet Italian sausage, casings removed

3 ribs celery, minced

2 medium carrots, minced

10 cloves fresh garlic, sliced

1 bunch broccoli rabe, washed, ends trimmed, and cut into bite-size pieces

Salt

2½ cups (600 ml) chicken broth, divided

2 large eggs

1 cup (100 g) grated Pecorino Romano cheese

Black pepper

1. Preheat the oven to 400°F (200°C). Grease a large casserole dish and a sheet of aluminum foil with butter.
2. Spread out the bread on 2 baking sheets. Bake the bread until dry, about 10 minutes. Remove from the oven and transfer to a large bowl.
3. In a large skillet with a lid, heat 2 tablespoons of the olive oil over medium heat. Add the sausage and break it up into small pieces with a wooden spoon. Cook, stirring occasionally, until the sausage has browned, 7 to 10 minutes. Using a slotted spoon, transfer it to a plate.
4. To the skillet, add the remaining 2 tablespoons olive oil, along with the celery, carrots, and garlic; cook, stirring occasionally, until the celery and carrots are slightly softened, about 5 minutes. Add the broccoli rabe and a generous sprinkle of salt; cook, stirring occasionally, until the broccoli rabe begins to wilt, 3 to 4 minutes. Add the sausage and ½ cup (120 ml) of the chicken broth. Cover and cook until the broccoli rabe has softened considerably and the liquid has evaporated, 8 to 10 minutes. Remove from the heat and add to the bowl with the bread.
5. In a medium bowl, whisk together the remaining 2 cups (480 ml) broth, the eggs, melted butter, cheese, and season with salt and pepper. Pour the mixture over the bread, little by little, while mixing with a spoon. It may appear dry at first but just keep mixing. Transfer the mixture to the prepared casserole dish and cover with the foil, buttered side down.
6. Bake for 20 minutes. Uncover and bake until the top is golden brown, about 20 minutes.

Nonna Liliana Barone's

GATTÒ DI PATATE

SICILIAN POTATO PIE

Prep time: 15 minutes
Cook time: 1 hour 30 minutes
Yield: 10 servings

A *gattò* is a savory potato pie layered with different meats and cheeses typical of the regions of Sicily and Campania. Nonna Liliana fills her *gattò* with savory *prosciutto cotto* and provolone, and makes it every Thanksgiving in place of mashed potatoes as a way of melding cultures.

Salt

5 pounds (2.3 kg) Idaho potatoes, washed and peeled

3 tablespoons extra-virgin olive oil, plus more for greasing and drizzling

¾ cup (180 ml) whole milk

½ cup (1 stick/120 g) unsalted butter, melted

¾ cup (75 g) grated Pecorino Romano cheese

3 large eggs, at room temperature

3 tablespoons chopped fresh parsley (optional)

¼ cup (30 g) plain bread crumbs, plus more for sprinkling

4 ounces (113 g) provolone cheese, sliced

4 ounces (113 g) sliced ham

8 ounces (225 g) fresh mozzarella cheese, sliced

1. Bring a large pot of generously salted water to a boil. Drop the potatoes in and cook until fork-tender, about 30 minutes.
2. Preheat the oven to 375°F (190°C). Grease a 9 by 13-inch (23 by 33 cm) baking dish with olive oil.
3. Drain and transfer the potatoes to a large bowl. While still warm, press the potatoes through a ricer and mix with a spatula until smooth. Add the milk, butter, and Pecorino Romano. Taste and season with salt as desired. Add the eggs and mix well.
4. To the prepared baking dish, sprinkle ¼ cup (30 g) bread crumbs over the bottom and sides and spread half of the potato mixture into an even layer. Top the potatoes with a layer of the provolone, a layer of the ham, and a layer of the mozzarella. Spread the remaining half of the potato mixture into an even layer on top. Using a fork, refine the surface and create some grooves. Drizzle some olive oil over the potatoes and sprinkle a thin coat of bread crumbs over the top.
5. Bake unti crispy on top, 45 to 60 minutes. Place the gattò under the broiler to give it a little color.

Nonna Rosa Carmelo's

PATATE DOLCI CON MIELE

HONEY SWEET POTATOES

Prep time: 5 minutes
Cook time: 45 minutes
Yield: 4 to 6 servings

Every Thanksgiving we must have Zia Rosa's honey sweet potatoes. In this super-easy recipe, Zia boils sliced sweet potatoes until "al dente," as she says, and then coats them with a honey and water emulsion before baking them until tender. Simple and delicious.

3 pounds (1.4 kg) sweet potatoes (about 3 medium potatoes), not peeled, scrubbed

¾ cup (255 g) honey

1. In a large pot, combine the sweet potatoes and enough cold water to cover completely. Cover the pot and bring to a boil over high heat. Cook until a fork only pierces the first inch (2.5 cm) or so of the potatoes, about 25 minutes. Drain and cool.
2. Once the sweet potatoes are cool enough to handle, peel and cut them into ½-inch-thick (13 mm) rounds and transfer them to a 9 by 13-inch (23 by 33 cm) baking dish, arranging them in an even layer.
3. Preheat the oven to 500°F (250°C).
4. In a small saucepan, bring the honey and ¾ cup (180 ml) of water to a boil over high heat. Pour the mixture over the potatoes.
5. Bake for 20 minutes, flipping the sweet potatoes halfway through the baking time.
6. Transfer the sweet potatoes to a serving dish and drizzle the liquid from the pan on top.

Nonna Romana Sciddurlo's

SALSA DI MIRTILLI ROSSI AL LIMONCELLO

CRANBERRY SAUCE WITH LIMONCELLO

Prep time: 5 minutes
Cook time: 16 minutes
Yield: 6 to 8 servings

Cranberry sauce is one of Nonna Romana's favorite things. "I love too much," she says every year as we pass the sauce around the table. While there's something incredibly nostalgic about canned cranberry sauce, it is very easy to make your own—just throw everything in a saucepan and simmer. It also allows you to control the sugar content and add flavors, such as limoncello, which gives this American classic a bit of Italian flair.

12 ounces (340 g) fresh cranberries
1 cup (200 g) sugar
Zest and juice of 1 orange
¼ teaspoon ground cinnamon
¼ cup (60 ml) limoncello liqueur

1. In a large saucepan, add the cranberries, sugar, orange zest and juice, and cinnamon. Cover the pan and bring the mixture to a boil over high heat, reduce the heat to low. Cook, uncovered, for 15 minutes, stirring occasionally with a wooden spoon.
2. Stir in the limoncello. Cook, stirring constantly, for 30 seconds to 1 minute. Remove from the heat and let cool to room temperature. The sauce will thicken slightly as it cools.

Nonna Romana Sciddurlo's

CROSTATA CON MIRTILLI ROSSI E MASCARPONE

NO-BAKE CRANBERRY AND MASCARPONE TART

Prep time: 2 hours
Cook time: 20 minutes
Yield: One 11-inch (28 cm) tart

Fun fact: Nonna Romana absolutely loves cranberry sauce (page 89)! She loves it so much that, together, we made it into this dessert. The topping for this effortlessly beautiful no-bake tart is super simple, and I'll let you in on a little secret: It's a great way to repurpose leftover cranberry sauce from Thanksgiving. If you can't find the vanilla cookies for the crust, vanilla wafers or graham crackers work as well.

TOPPING

12 ounces (340 g) cranberries, fresh or frozen

⅔ cup (150 g) packed brown sugar

½ cup (120 ml) freshly squeezed orange juice

¼ cup (60 ml) Cointreau or another orange-flavored liqueur

Zest of 1 orange, plus more for garnishing (optional)

1 cinnamon stick (3 inches/7.5 cm)

¼ cup (36 g) toasted almonds, coarsely chopped

CRUST

12 ounces (340 g) Stella D'oro Margherite Vanilla cookies

½ cup (1 stick/120 g) unsalted butter, melted

FILLING

1½ cups (350 ml) heavy whipping cream

¾ cup (90 g) confectioners' sugar

16 ounces (455 g) mascarpone cheese, at room temperature

1. **To make the topping:** In a small saucepan, bring the cranberries, brown sugar, orange juice, Cointreau, orange zest, and cinnamon stick to a boil over medium-high heat. Reduce the heat to medium and cook, stirring occasionally, until the cranberries pop and the mixture becomes smooth, 15 to 20 minutes. Set aside to cool.
2. **To make the crust:** In a food processor fitted with the blade attachment, process the cookies until fine. Add the melted butter and process until the mixture resembles sand. Press the crumbs into an 11-inch (28 cm) loose-bottomed tart pan and refrigerate.
3. **Meanwhile, make the filling:** In a large bowl, using an electric handheld mixture, beat the heavy cream and confectioners' sugar at high speed until stiff peaks form.
4. In another large bowl, place the mascarpone. Using a rubber spatula, gently fold in the whipped cream. Transfer the mixture to the crust and smooth it out with the spatula. Refrigerate until the filling is set, 1 to 2 hours.
5. Spoon the cranberry topping over the tart before serving. Sprinkle with the toasted almonds and orange zest, if desired.

Nonna Romana Sciddurlo's

TIRAMISÙ A L LA ZUCCA

PUMPKIN TIRAMISU

Prep time: 4 hours 20 minutes
Yield: 8 to 10 servings

Tiramisu is a beloved Italian dessert. It's smooth, creamy, and caffeinated, so what's not to like? Nonna Romana and I love making this pumpkin version for the holidays, primarily because it's no-bake. Let's be honest, we're all trying to find an easy and delicious way to make something special for big gatherings. You can leave out the amaretto or substitute it with a touch of almond extract to make it alcohol-free.

FILLING

2 cups (480 ml) heavy whipping cream

2 tablespoons confectioners' sugar

16 ounces (455 g) mascarpone cheese, at room temperature

1 can (15 ounces/425 g) pure pumpkin (not pumpkin pie filling)

½ cup (120 g) packed brown sugar

2 teaspoons pumpkin pie spice

CRUST

2¼ cups (540 ml) brewed espresso coffee

¾ cup (180 ml) amaretto liqueur or almond extract to taste

¼ cup (60 ml) whole milk

48 to 50 ladyfinger cookies or savoiardi

TOPPING

1 tablespoon granulated sugar

1 tablespoon ground cinnamon

1. **To make the filling:** In a large bowl, using a handheld electric mixer, beat the heavy cream and confectioners' sugar at high speed until stiff peaks form.
2. In another large bowl, gently fold together the mascarpone, pumpkin, brown sugar, and pumpkin pie spice until smooth and well combined. (Be gentle while mixing the mascarpone because it has a tendency to curdle and become a bit grainy if it's overworked.) Gently fold the whipped cream into the pumpkin mixture until smooth and airy.
3. **To make the crust:** In a shallow dish, combine the espresso, amaretto, and milk. Working one at a time, dip each ladyfinger into the coffee mixture, transferring them to a 9 by 13-inch (23 by 33 cm) baking dish, creating an even layer (break the cookies to fit, if necessary). Spoon one-third of the filling over the first layer of cookies. Repeat twice more.
4. **To make the topping:** In a small bowl, combine the granulated sugar and cinnamon. Sprinkle it over the top layer. Refrigerate for at least 4 hours or up to overnight. Serve chilled.

Nonna Rosa Carmelo's

CROSTATA DI ZUCCA ALL'AMARETTO

AMARETTO PUMPKIN PIE

Prep time: 10 minutes

Cook time: 1 hour 30 minutes

Yield: One 9-inch (23 cm) pie

CRUST

Butter, for greasing

4 ounces (113 g) amaretti cookies, plus cookie crumbs for garnishing

¼ cup (30 g) all-purpose or 00 flour

2 tablespoons slivered almonds

1 tablespoon packed brown sugar

1 teaspoon ground cinnamon

Pinch salt

½ cup (1 stick/120 g) salted butter, melted

FILLING

8 ounces (225 g) almond paste

1 can (15 ounces/425 g) pure pumpkin (not pumpkin pie filling)

1 cup (240 ml) heavy whipping cream

½ cup (120 g) packed brown sugar

3 tablespoons amaretto liqueur

2 large eggs

1 packet (½ ounce/15 g) Italian vanilla powder or 1 teaspoon vanilla extract

2 teaspoons pumpkin pie spice

AMARETTO WHIPPED CREAM

1 cup (240 ml) heavy whipping cream

1 tablespoon amaretto liqueur

1 tablespoon confectioners' sugar

Splash vanilla extract

No Thanksgiving would be complete without a delicious pumpkin pie. My Zia Rosa was introduced to this iconic American dessert in 1966, when her American-born sister-in-law brought it over for Thanksgiving dinner. Over the years, Zia Rosa "Italianized" the classic filling with the addition of a splash of the amaretto liqueur. The crust has evolved as well, with the addition of almonds for crunch and sweet amaretto cookies replacing the graham crackers. The final touch is a dollop of amaretto-spiked whipped cream spread generously over the top to create the perfect Italian-American confection.

1. Preheat the oven to 350°F (180°C). Grease a 9-inch (23 cm) pie plate with butter.
2. **To make the crust:** In a food processor fitted with the blade attachment, process the amaretti cookies, flour, almonds, brown sugar, cinnamon, and salt until finely ground, about 20 seconds. Drizzle in the melted butter and process until the mixture resembles wet sand. Press the crumbs into the prepared pie plate, using the bottom of a glass to create a smooth crust. Bake until the edges begin to color, 10 to 12 minutes.
3. Remove the crust from the oven and, while it's still hot, use the back of a spoon to further smooth it out and push it up the sides of the pie plate. Set aside to cool.
4. **Meanwhile, make the filling:** In a large bowl, using a large cheese grater, grate the almond paste. Add the pumpkin. With a handheld electric mixer, mix at high speed until fully incorporated and smooth. Add the heavy cream, brown sugar, amaretto, eggs, vanilla, and pumpkin pie spice; mix at high speed until well combined. Transfer the filling to the prepared crust.
5. Bake until the edges are fully set but the center is still wobbly, 1 hour to 1 hour and 15 minutes. Turn off the oven and let the pie cool completely in the oven, with the oven door slightly open, to help prevent cracks.
6. **To make the amaretto whipped cream:** In a large bowl, combine the heavy whipping cream, amaretto, confectioners' sugar, and vanilla. Beat with a handheld electric mixer until soft peaks form. Spread the whipped cream over the cooled pie and garnish with amaretti cookie crumbs.

Nonna Romana Sciddurlo's

BISCOTTI DI RICOTTA E ZUCCA

PUMPKIN RICOTTA COOKIES

Prep time: 10 minutes

Cook time: 15 minutes

Yield: About 40 cookies

There is an unwritten rule that cookies must be made for every Italian-American holiday. Okay, I just made that up, but who's to say there isn't? It's unwritten! These pumpkin ricotta cookies are a spiced-up version of Nonna Romana's classic ricotta cookies and are melt-in-your-mouth deliciousness. Nonna Romana will sometimes serve these without the cinnamon-sugar glaze, as they're perfect for dipping in her morning coffee!

COOKIES

2 cups (240 g) all-purpose or 00 flour

2 teaspoons pumpkin pie spice

1 teaspoon baking powder

½ teaspoon salt

½ cup (1 stick/120 g) unsalted butter, at room temperature

1 cup (225 g) packed brown sugar

8 ounces (225 g) ricotta

4 ounces (113 g) canned pure pumpkin (not pumpkin pie filling)

1 teaspoon vanilla extract

1 large egg

GLAZE

2 cups (240 g) confectioners' sugar

2 tablespoons milk

¼ teaspoon ground cinnamon

1. **To make the cookies:** Preheat the oven to 350°F (180°C). Line 2 baking sheets with parchment paper or aluminum foil.
2. In a large bowl, whisk together the flour, pumpkin pie spice, baking powder, and salt.
3. In the bowl of a stand mixer fitted with the paddle attachment, beat the butter and brown sugar at medium speed until fluffy, about 5 minutes. Add the ricotta, pumpkin, vanilla, and egg. Mix at medium-high speed until well combined. With the mixer at low speed, add the dry ingredients a little at a time. Continue mixing at low speed until the flour is absorbed and a dough forms.
4. Using a tablespoon to measure (15 g each), roll the dough into balls and place them about 2 inches (5 cm) apart on the prepared baking sheets. Bake until the cookies are very lightly golden, about 15 minutes. Transfer the cookies to a wire rack to cool. Let cool completely before icing.
5. **To make the glaze:** In a small bowl, whisk together the confectioners' sugar, milk, and cinnamon until smooth. Dip the cookies into the glaze and place them on a wire rack to dry.

Nonna Romana Sciddurlo's

TORTA DI MELE E RICOTTA

APPLE CINNAMON RICOTTA CAKE

Prep time: 10 minutes
Cook time: 1 hour
Yield: One 9-inch (23 cm) cake

When it comes to Thanksgiving desserts, Nonna Romana likes to jazz up the classic recipes in her repertoire. She has made so many versions of this humble olive oil and ricotta cake, but this one really brings out the essence of the holiday. The aroma of sweet apple-cinnamon goodness will fill your home from top to bottom. Should there be any leftovers (which isn't likely), this cake works beautifully as a breakfast cake with coffee in the morning.

Nonstick cooking spray, for greasing
4 large eggs
1½ cups (375 g) whole-milk ricotta
1 cup (200 g) granulated sugar
1 teaspoon vanilla extract
¾ cup (180 ml) olive oil
Zest of 1 orange
2 teaspoons ground cinnamon
2 cups (240 g) all-purpose or 00 flour
1 tablespoon baking powder
3 Gala apples, 2 cut into 1-inch (2.5 cm) chunks and 1 thinly sliced
Confectioners' sugar, for dusting

1 Preheat the oven to 350°F (180°C). Grease a 9-inch (23 cm) springform pan with cooking spray.

2 In a large bowl, stir together the eggs, ricotta, granulated sugar, and vanilla. Add the olive oil, orange zest, and cinnamon and stir to combine. Stir in the flour and baking powder, a little at a time, mixing until fully combined. Fold in the apple chunks.

3 Transfer the batter to the prepared pan. Arrange the sliced apples on top and sprinkle with confectioners' sugar. Bake until the apples are golden, about 1 hour. Serve at room temperature.

CHRISTMAS EVE

Nonna Rosa Vella's

RISO ALLA MARINARA

LIVORNESE SEAFOOD RICE

Prep time: 20 minutes

Cook time: 1 hour 15 minutes

Yield: 6 servings

Christmas Eve at Nonna Rosa's house isn't complete without this seafood rice on the table. This specialty from Livorno is very similar to its Neapolitan cousin, the famous *risotto alla pescatora* (seafood risotto), with a few differences. The rice is baked in the oven instead of cooked on the stovetop, and the blend of seafood is cooked separately. Both components are then combined with butter in a process called *mantecare*, which is used in classic risotto preparation to cream the ingredients together.

- 24 mussels, scrubbed and debearded
- 2 pounds (910 g) cockles or 24 littleneck clams, scrubbed and rinsed
- 2 pounds (910 g) large shrimp, peeled, deveined, and cut into 1-inch (2.5 cm) pieces
- 2 pounds (910 g) calamari, cleaned, bodies cut into 1-inch (2.5 cm) rings, and tentacles cut into 1-inch (2.5 cm) pieces
- 3½ cups (28 ounces/840 ml) beef broth
- 3½ cups (28 ounces/840 ml) chicken broth
- 5 tablespoons extra-virgin olive oil
- 10 cloves garlic, minced
- ½ teaspoon red pepper flakes
- ½ cup (30 g) chopped fresh parsley
- 16 ounces (455 g) long-grain white rice, rinsed
- ½ cup (1 stick/120 g) salted butter

1. Line a fine-mesh strainer with a piece of cheesecloth and have a medium bowl handy. Heat a large skillet with a lid over medium-high heat. Add the mussels, cover, and steam until the mussels open, 5 to 7 minutes. Discard any mussels that have not opened. Remove the meat from the shells and transfer to a large bowl. Discard the shells. Into the medium bowl, strain the mussel broth from the pan through the prepared strainer.
2. Return the skillet to medium heat and add the cockles, cover, and steam until they open, 3 to 5 minutes. Discard any cockles that have not opened. Remove the meat from the shells and transfer to the bowl with the mussels. Discard the shells. Strain the cockle broth from the pan through the prepared strainer into the bowl with the mussel broth.
3. In a large saucepan, add the shrimp and enough cold running water to just cover them; bring to a boil over high heat and cook for 10 minutes. Reserve 1 cup (240 ml) of the cooking water. Drain the shrimp and add them to the bowl with the mussels and clams.
4. In the same saucepan, add the calamari and enough cold running water to just cover them; bring to a boil over high heat and cook for 10 minutes. Reserve 1 cup (240 ml) of the cooking water. Drain the calamari and add them to the bowl with the rest of the seafood.
5. Preheat the oven to 400°F (200°C).
6. In a small stockpot, bring the beef and chicken broths to a boil over high heat, then remove from the heat.

CONTINUED ON PAGE 100

CONTINUED FROM PAGE 99

7 In a large skillet, heat the olive oil over medium heat. Add the garlic, red pepper flakes, and parsley; cook, stirring occasionally, for 1 minute. Reduce the heat to low. Add the rice and stir until it's coated in oil and lightly toasted, 2 to 3 minutes. Add about 4½ cups (1 L) of the warmed broth; stir until absorbed. Keep the remaining broth warm on the stove while the rice bakes.

8 In a 9 by 13-inch (23 by 33 cm) baking dish, spread the rice in an even layer. Cover with aluminum foil and bake for 20 minutes. Check on the rice halfway through: If it looks too dry, add some of the reserved broth; the rice should be tender but still have some bite to it. Remove from the oven and let cool for 5 minutes.

9 In the same skillet used for the rice, melt the butter over medium heat. Add the rice and stir until it's coated it in the butter. Add the mussels, clams, shrimp, calamari, the reserved shellfish broth, and the reserved shrimp and calamari cooking water; cook, stirring constantly with a wooden spoon to prevent sticking until half the liquid is absorbed and the rice is perfectly tender, 10 to 12 minutes. Serve immediately.

Nonna Rosa Says

The consistency of the rice can be a little tricky to master in this dish. Check the rice often to make sure there is enough broth, or the rice can become tough.

Nonna Romana Sciddurlo's

BACCALÀ FRITTO

FRIED BACCALÀ

Prep time: 15 minutes, plus 1 to 3 days soaking

Cook time: 20 minutes

Yield: 4 to 6 servings

If you visit Nonna Romana in her Brooklyn basement apartment anytime between the day after Thanksgiving and Christmas Eve, there's a good chance you'll be met with the warm and intoxicating aroma of fried baccalà. It's no secret that baccalà, or salt cod, is an integral part of Christmas in an Italian household. Though it requires a bit of preparation, many Italians view it as a ritual or tradition. Nonna Romana's favorite way to prepare it is to batter it in a traditional Pugliese *pastella* (batter) full of garlic, mint, and cheese, and fry it until it's golden brown and crispy on the outside.

- 1½ pounds (680 g) baccalà (salt cod)
- 2 large eggs
- ½ cup (50 g) grated Pecorino Romano cheese
- 4 cloves garlic, minced
- 1 tablespoon minced fresh parsley
- 1 teaspoon salt
- 1 cup (124 g) all-purpose or 00 flour
- Oil, for frying

1. In a large bowl, add the baccalà and enough cold water to cover it. Place the bowl in the refrigerator and change the water 3 times a day; repeat for 1 to 3 days, depending on saltiness. Drain and pat dry with a paper towel, then cut the baccalà into 3- to 4-inch (7.5 to 10 cm) pieces.
2. In a medium bowl, whisk together the eggs, cheese, garlic, parsley, and salt. Whisk in the flour until absorbed. Whisk in 1 cup (240 ml) of water until smooth. The batter should fall from the whisk in ribbons.
3. In a medium heavy-bottomed skillet, heat about 1½ inches (4 cm) of oil over high heat. Working with 1 piece at a time, dip the baccalà into the batter, letting the excess fall back into the bowl. Carefully add it to the hot oil and fry, in batches, until golden, 3 to 5 minutes per side. Fry any leftover batter to make fritters. Serve immediately.

Nonna Michelina Gagliardo's

BACCALÀ GHIOTTA

SALT COD WITH POTATOES

Prep time: 15 minutes, plus 1 to 3 days soaking

Cook time: 55 minutes

Yield: 4 to 6 servings

BACCALÀ

1½ pounds (680 g) baccalà (salt cod)

Oil, for frying

All-purpose or 00 flour, for dredging

SAUCE

¼ cup (60 ml) extra-virgin olive oil

1 medium onion, cut into ¼-inch (6 mm) dice

3 ribs celery, cut into ½-inch (13 mm) dice

1 cup (155 g) Kalamata or Gaeta olives, pitted

1 can (28 ounces/794 g) crushed tomatoes

3 small russet potatoes, peeled and cut into 1-inch (2.5 cm) cubes

2 tablespoons capers, rinsed

Salt

16 ounces (455 g) dried mezzi rigatoni

At Zia Michelina's house in the Bronx, baccalà is fried and then cooked in a hearty tomato sauce, until the fried baccalà pieces are beautifully tender, or as Zia Michelina would say, "*Molto* beautiful, baby!" The leftover sauce is tossed with pasta, because "you no waste nothing!"

1. **To make the baccalà:** In a large bowl, add the baccalà and enough cold water to cover it. Place the bowl in the refrigerator and change the water 3 times a day; repeat for 1 to 3 days, depending on saltiness. Drain and pat dry with a paper towel, then cut the baccalà into 3- to 4-inch (7.5 to 10 cm) pieces.
2. Line a plate with paper towels. In a medium heavy-bottomed skillet, heat 1 inch (2.5 cm) of oil over high heat.
3. Place the flour in a shallow dish and dredge the baccalà pieces in the flour. Carefully add them to the hot oil and, working in batches, fry until golden, 3 to 5 minutes per side. Transfer to the prepared plate.
4. **To make the sauce:** In a large saucepan with a lid, heat the olive oil over medium heat. Add the onion, celery, and olives and cook, stirring occasionally, until the onion is translucent and the celery is soft, 5 to 7 minutes. Add the tomatoes. Fill the empty tomato can three-fourths full of water, swish it around, and add the tomato water to the pan. Add the potatoes and bring the mixture to a boil over high heat and cook for 5 minutes. Reduce the heat to low, cover the pan, and let the sauce simmer for 15 to 20 minutes.
5. Add the capers and fried baccalà to the sauce. Cook, covered, for 5 minutes. Transfer the baccalà to a plate, leaving the sauce in the pan.
6. Bring a medium stockpot of generously salted water to a boil over high heat. Drop in the pasta and cook until al dente. Drain and add the pasta to the sauce. Increase the heat to medium-high and cook, tossing to coat the pasta, for 1 to 2 minutes.
7. Serve in warm bowls with pieces of the baccalà broken up on top of the pasta, or as a first course with the baccalà served as a second course.

Nonna Lorella Colandrea's

INSALATA DI POLPO

OCTOPUS SALAD

Prep time: 4 hours

Cook time: 45 minutes

Yield: 4 servings

Nonna Lorella dresses her salad with super-simple, clean flavors, so the octopus can be the star of the show. Some people may be intimidated by the prospect of cooking an octopus, but it's much easier than you think. Instead of one large octopus, try and buy a few octopi that are smaller in size, which will be much more tender.

OCTOPUS

3 pounds (1.4 kg) octopus (see Nonna Lorella Says)

1 medium Idaho potato, washed and not peeled

2 ribs celery, cut into ½-inch (13 mm) dice

DRESSING

3 cloves garlic, minced

⅔ cup (160 ml) extra-virgin olive oil

Juice of 3 lemons

1 tablespoon white wine

Salt and black pepper

1. **To cook the octopus:** Clean the octopus under cold running water. Bring a large stockpot filled with about 14 cups (3.3 L) of water to a boil over medium-high heat. You want enough water to cover the octopus completely. Add the potato to the pot. (According to Nonna lore, if you boil a potato with octopus, when the potato is tender, the octopus will also be tender.)
2. Hold the octopus by the head and plunge it, tentacles first, 3 times into the boiling water before dropping it into the pot. Let the water return to a boil and cook until both the octopus and the potato are fork-tender, 30 to 45 minutes. Drain and transfer to a bowl. Discard the potato. Let the octopus cool to room temperature.
3. Cut the cooled octopus into 1-inch (2.5 cm) pieces and place them in a large bowl. Add the diced celery to the bowl.
4. **To make the dressing:** In a small bowl, whisk together the garlic, olive oil, lemon juice, and wine. Pour the dressing over the octopus and celery and toss to coat evenly. Season with salt and pepper to taste.
5. Refrigerate for at least 4 hours or up to overnight before serving. This can be made up to 2 days in advance.

Nonna Lorella Says

I recommend using frozen octopus because the octopus becomes more tender during the freezing process, and the eyes and beak will most likely have been removed. If using fresh octopus, you will need to clean the inside of the head thoroughly and remove the eyes and beak.

Nonna Lorella Colandrea's

SPAGHETTI DI NATALE

SPAGHETTI WITH NUTS, RAISINS, AND ANCHOVIES

Prep time: 5 minutes
Cook time: 25 minutes
Yield: 4 to 6 servings

A dinner at Nonna Lorella's house is always an event. Everyone is always singing Neapolitan love songs, telling stories, and sipping bottomless glasses of wine, and that's just on a Tuesday! Christmas Eve is even livelier, and usually goes well into the early morning hours. Their feast tends to begin a little later in the evening, because most of her family is in the restaurant business. So this super-quick and flavorful pasta dish is a no-brainer. The spaghetti spends most of the time cooking directly in a sauce chock-full of raisins, pine nuts, olives, and walnuts, which allows it to perfectly absorb the sweet and savory flavors. As Nonna Lorella says, "*Na cosa sciue sciue, ma buona*! (Something super quick, but good!)"

Salt
¾ cup (180 ml) extra-virgin olive oil
3 cloves garlic, sliced
⅓ cup (33 g) walnuts
⅓ cup (45 g) pignoli (pine nuts)
7 or 8 anchovy fillets
⅓ cup (50 g) currants or raisins
1 cup (155 g) Kalamata or Gaeta olives, pitted
½ cup (121 g) canned crushed tomatoes
16 ounces (455 g) dried spaghetti

1. Bring a medium stockpot of generously salted water to a boil over high heat.
2. Heat a large skillet over medium heat and add the olive oil, garlic, walnuts, pignoli, and anchovies. Cook, stirring occasionally, until the anchovies melt and the garlic is golden, 3 to 4 minutes. Stir in the currants and olives and cook for 1 to 2 minutes. Add the tomatoes and reduce the heat to low. Cook, stirring occasionally, for 5 minutes.
3. Meanwhile, drop the pasta into the boiling water and cook for half the time indicated on the package, 5 to 6 minutes. The pasta will still be quite hard. Scoop out 2½ cups (600 ml) of pasta water and add it to the tomato sauce. Drain the spaghetti and add it to the sauce.
4. Increase the heat to medium-high. Cook, tossing the pasta, until the sauce reduces and no longer pools at the bottom of the pan, and the pasta is al dente, 7 to 10 minutes. Season with salt to taste.

Nonna Giuseppa Valenti Cocciola's

INSALATA DI MARE

SEVEN FISHES SEAFOOD SALAD

Prep time: 3 hours, plus 1 to 3 days soaking

Cook time: 1 hour 50 minutes

Yield: 8 to 10 servings

Okay, so this recipe can be a labor of love, but every single bite will be absolutely worth it (if you manage to get some on your plate)! No matter how much seafood salad Nonna Giuseppa makes, there never seems to be enough to go around. She makes it every Christmas Eve as part of her legendary Feast of the Seven Fishes, but it's so light and refreshing that it works beautifully as a summer antipasto as well.

SEAFOOD

1 pound (455 g) baccalà (salt cod)

½ cup (120 ml) dry white wine

3 pounds (1.4 kg) mussels, scrubbed and debearded

1 pound (455 g) calamari, cleaned, bodies cut into ½-inch (13 mm) rings, and tentacles left whole

1 pound (455 g) small scallops

1 pound (455 g) shrimp, washed, peeled, and deveined

1 pound (455 g) *scungilli* (whelk)

1 pound (455 g) tenderized octopus

BROTH

3 cloves garlic

3 bay leaves

12 black peppercorns

1 teaspoon fennel seeds

1 tablespoon minced fresh parsley

Peel of ½ lemon

½ cup (120 ml) dry white wine

1 tablespoon salt

1. **To prepare the seafood:** In a large bowl, add the baccalà and enough cold water to cover it. Place the bowl in the refrigerator and change the water 3 times a day; repeat for 1 to 3 days, depending on saltiness. Drain and shred into bite-size pieces.
2. Line a fine-mesh strainer with a piece of cheesecloth and have a medium bowl handy. Heat a large heavy-bottomed saucepan with a lid over medium heat. Add the wine and mussels and cook, covered, until the mussels open and the meat is detached from the shell, about 10 minutes. Discard any mussels that have not opened. Remove the meat from the shells and set aside. Discard the shells. Into the medium bowl, strain the mussel broth from the pan through the prepared strainer.
3. **To make the broth and cook the seafood:** Fill a small double boiler halfway with water. (If you don't have a double boiler, a regular stockpot can be used with a large strainer or colander to scoop out the fish.) Add the garlic, bay leaves, peppercorns, fennel seeds, parsley, lemon peel, white wine, and salt and bring to a boil over high heat.
4. To the boiling water, add the baccalà and cook for 6 to 7 minutes; remove it from the water and set aside. Let the water return to a boil. Add the calamari and cook for 4 to 5 minutes; remove them from the water and set aside. Let the water return to a boil. Add the scallops and cook for 4 to 5 minutes; remove them from the water and set aside. Let the water return to a boil. Add the shrimp and cook until pink and tender, 6 to 7 minutes (depending on the size); remove them from the water and set aside.

CONTINUED ON PAGE 108

CONTINUED FROM PAGE 107

SALAD

2 ribs celery, cut into ½-inch (13 mm) dice

½ cup (30 g) chopped fresh parsley

2 medium carrots, grated

1 cup (192 g) green olives with pimento

1 cup (240 ml) freshly squeezed lemon juice

¾ cup (180 ml) extra-virgin olive oil

12 cloves garlic, minced

1 tablespoon white wine vinegar

Dash dried oregano

Salt

Red pepper flakes (optional)

5 Let the water return to a boil. Add the scungilli to the pot and cook until firm but tender, 10 to 15 minutes. Remove them from the pot and set aside. Let the water return to a boil. Finally, add the octopus, dip the colander in and out 2 times, and then let the octopus cook until the body is tender and the tentacles have curled, about 20 minutes. Remove it from the pot and set aside.

6 On a cutting board, remove the scungilli from their shells and cut them into ½-inch (13 mm) pieces. Cut the octopus into ½-inch (13 mm) pieces.

7 **To assemble:** To a large bowl, add the baccalà, mussels, calamari, scallops, shrimp, scungilli, octopus, celery, parsley, carrots, and olives and toss well.

8 To a medium bowl, whisk together the lemon juice, olive oil, garlic, vinegar, dried oregano, salt to taste, red pepper flakes (if using), and the reserved mussel broth. Drizzle the mixture over the seafood and vegetables and toss well. Cover the bowl and refrigerate for at least 3 hours or up to overnight. The salad can be chilled for up to 2 days.

Nonna Giuseppa Says

Feel free to change up the seafood depending on your taste. Lobster is a special and delicious addition. When I'm making this for Christmas, I always make the salad a day or two before so the flavors intensify.

Nonna Carmela D'angelo's

CARDONI FRITTI

FRIED CARDOONS

Prep time: 15 minutes
Cook time: 45 minutes
Yield: 8 to 10 servings

Every holiday season, Nonna Carmela and her grandson John take a trip to Arthur Avenue in the Bronx to shop for ingredients for Christmas. One of their first stops is for fresh cardoons. A cardoon is a giant edible thistle with stalks that resemble bunches of celery, related to the artichoke plant; instead of the flower, we eat the stalks. "These are a lot of work," she says, "but every year they all ask for them, so as long as I'm here I'll do it." When prepared Nonna Carmela's way, the whole plate is in danger before they're even served. "I have to hide them!" she says with a wink and a smile. I believe her.

- 1½ pounds (680 g) cardoons
- All-purpose or 00 flour, for dredging
- 4 large eggs
- 2 tablespoons whole milk
- 1 cup (115 g) plain bread crumbs
- 1 tablespoon chopped fresh parsley
- ¼ cup (25 g) grated Parmigiano-Reggiano cheese
- 2 cloves garlic, minced
- 1 teaspoon salt
- ¼ teaspoon black pepper
- Olive oil, for frying

1. Discard any brown or discolored leaves and smaller stalks from the cardoons. Trim the base of the cardoons to break up the bunch and make individual stalks. Using a vegetable peeler, peel the outer fibrous strings off each rib as you would with celery.
2. Cut the stalks crosswise into 4- to 5-inch (10 to 13 cm) pieces and transfer to a bowl of water to prevent oxidation. Drain the water and rinse the cardoons well under cold running water.
3. To a small stockpot, add the cardoons and enough cold water to cover them. Bring to a boil over high heat, then reduce the heat to low. Simmer until tender and easily pierced with a knife, 20 to 30 minutes. Drain and transfer to a plate.
4. Place the flour in a shallow dish. In another shallow dish, whisk together the eggs and milk. In a third shallow dish, combine the bread crumbs, parsley, cheese, garlic, salt, and pepper.
5. Line a plate with paper towels. In a large skillet, heat about 1½ inches (4 cm) of olive oil over medium-high heat.
6. Dredge each cardoon in the flour, then in the beaten egg, and then in the bread-crumb mixture. Working in batches, place the coated cardoons in the hot oil and fry, turning frequently, until golden brown, 2 to 3 minutes. Transfer to the prepared plate. Serve warm.

Nonna Lorella Colandrea's

PIZZA DI SCAROLA

ESCAROLE PIE

Prep time: 35 minutes
Cook time: 1 hour 25 minutes
Yield: 6 to 8 servings

There is a saying according to a Neapolitan Christmas tradition, "*la vigilia è di magro* (the eve must be light)." There is usually no meat consumed on Christmas Eve at Nonna Lorella's house. Just a "light" snack, if you will, of several courses of seafood and vegetables. And, of course, her classic pizza, an exquisite escarole pie bursting with olives, raisins, and nuts. She rolls out her crust with a pasta roller to get it super thin, allowing it to virtually "fry" in the oven.

FILLING

3 teaspoons salt, divided

3 heads escarole, ends trimmed, washed, and cut into 1-inch (2.5 cm) strips

4 cloves garlic, minced

½ cup (50 g) walnuts, coarsely chopped

½ cup (78 g) Kalamata olives, pitted and coarsely chopped

¼ cup (35 g) raisins

¼ cup (34 g) pignoli (pine nuts)

5 tablespoons extra-virgin olive oil

3 or 4 anchovy fillets

DOUGH

3 cups (360 g) all-purpose or 00 flour

½ teaspoon baking soda

½ teaspoon baking powder

½ teaspoon salt

Dash black pepper

1 cup (240 ml) warm water

1 tablespoon apple cider vinegar

1 cup (240 ml) extra-virgin olive oil, divided, plus more for brushing

1. **To make the filling:** Bring a large pot of water with 2 teaspoons of the salt to a boil over high heat. Add the escarole, reduce the heat to medium-low, cover the pot, and cook for 30 minutes.
2. Drain the escarole and run it under cold water. Squeeze out the excess water then transfer it to a large bowl. Add the garlic, walnuts, olives, raisins, pignoli, olive oil, the remaining 1 teaspoon salt, and the anchovies. Mix well.
3. **To make the dough:** In a medium bowl, whisk together the flour, baking soda, baking powder, salt, and pepper.
4. In the bowl of a stand mixer fitted with the dough hook attachment, add the warm water, vinegar, and ½ cup (120 ml) of the olive oil; mix at medium speed for 1 minute. Add the flour mixture and mix at medium speed until a smooth ball of dough begins to form, 3 to 5 minutes.
5. Preheat the oven to 400°F (200°C).
6. Lightly flour a work surface and turn the dough out on to it. Roll the dough into a log about 12 inches (30 cm) long and cut it into 6 equal pieces. Take 4 pieces of the dough and, using a pasta press stand mixer attachment set on the #1 setting, pass each piece of dough through the pasta press 2 or 3 times. Change to the #2 setting and pass the dough through the press 2 or 3 more times, until you have smooth sheets at least 12 inches (30 cm) long, then lay them in a 12-inch (30 cm) aluminum oven-safe skillet, overlapping one another by at least 1 inch (2.5 cm). Let any excess hang over the sides. Spread the filling over the sheets in an even layer, leaving about a 1-inch (2.5 cm) border.

7. Roll out the remaining 2 pieces of dough as in step 6. Place them over the filling in the center of the skillet, overlapping each other by at least 1 inch (2.5 cm). Fold the excess dough over the filling so it just meets the top 2 pieces of dough. Trim any excess and patch any holes with the trimmed pieces. This will end up being the bottom of the pizza, so it doesn't have to be perfect. Dock with a fork and brush evenly with the remaining ½ cup (120 ml) olive oil.
8. Bake for 35 minutes. Wearing oven mitts on both hands, remove the skillet from the oven. Place a large dinner plate over the skillet. Place your hand over the plate and quickly flip the pizza onto the plate. Slide the pizza back into the skillet and brush with a bit of extra olive oil. Bake until the crust is firm and golden brown, about 20 minutes. Let the pizza cool in the pan for about 15 minutes before sliding it onto a plate. Let cool to room temperature before cutting into slices and serving.

Nonna Romana Sciddurlo's

CAVATELLI AI FRUTTI DI MARE

SEAFOOD CAVATELLI

Prep time: 15 minutes

Cook time: 35 minutes

Yield: 4 to 6 servings

This incredibly versatile seafood pasta packs in all the flavor. *Frutti di mare* literally translates to "fruits of the sea," so feel free to mix up the combination of seafood for your Feast of the Seven Fishes. Nonna Romana loves to serve this with cavatelli, as the little "cave" shape of the pasta perfectly absorbs the sauce.

18 littleneck clams

1½ pounds (680 g) live lobster

¼ cup (60 ml) extra-virgin olive oil, divided

Salt

16 ounces (455 g) cavatelli pasta, preferably homemade

4 cloves garlic, sliced

Red pepper flakes

10 cherry tomatoes, halved

½ cup (120 ml) white wine

2 tablespoons (8 g) minced fresh parsley, divided

½ pound (225 g) large shrimp, washed and deveined

1. Shuck the clams with a bowl underneath to catch the juice. Transfer the meat to a small bowl. Strain the clam juice through a fine-mesh strainer lined with cheesecloth. Alternatively, heat a medium stockpot with a lid over medium heat and add the clams. Cover and cook just until the clams begin to open, about 2 minutes. (You don't want to cook them, just open the shells.) Transfer the meat to a small bowl and strain the clam juice.
2. Place the lobster on a cutting board, belly side up with the tail closest to you. With a large chef's knife or cleaver, halve the lobster lengthwise, beginning at the head and splitting down the tail. Separate the claws from the arms. Chop the arms in pieces and set aside. Chop the lobster halves into 2-inch (5 cm) pieces and set aside.
3. In a large skillet, heat 2 tablespoons of the olive oil over medium-high heat. Add all the lobster pieces to the pan, meat side down, and sear until the meat is firm, about 5 minutes. Transfer the lobster to a plate.
4. Bring a medium stockpot of salted water to a boil over high heat. Drop the cavatelli into the boiling water. Cook until al dente. Drain.
5. In the skillet, heat the remaining 2 tablespoons olive oil over medium-high heat. Add the garlic, and red pepper flakes to taste and cook, stirring occasionally, until the garlic just begins to turn golden, about 30 seconds. Add the tomatoes and cook, stirring occasionally, for 2 to 3 minutes. Add the wine and cook, stirring occasionally, until the alcohol evaporates, 2 to 3 minutes. Add the juice from the clams and let the mixture come to a boil. Add the lobster pieces and 1 tablespoon of the parsley; cook, stirring occasionally, for 2 minutes. Add the shrimp and clams; cook, stirring occasionally, until the shrimp are pink and the clams are firm, 6 to 7 minutes. Season with salt to taste. Add the cavatelli and cook, tossing, for 2 minutes. Sprinkle with the remaining 1 tablespoon parsley and serve.

Nonna Rosa Vella's

CACCIUCCO LIVORNESE

LIVORNESE FISH STEW

Prep time: 20 minutes
Cook time: 2 hours
Yield: 6 to 8 servings

This Tuscan seafood stew used to be made by poor fishermen as a way to utilize fish that didn't sell. Nonna Rosa remembers her trips as a girl to the mercato centrale in Livorno, where her mother would send her and her sisters to buy fish for a cacciucco that would feed their family of ten. "They were all fishes you don't see too much today. Palombo, gallinella, pesce prete, cicale. Maybe we didn't appreciate them then because they were all we had, but the flavors were so good!"

- 3 tablespoons extra-virgin olive oil, plus more for drizzling
- 9 cloves garlic, divided
- ½ teaspoon red pepper flakes
- 5 fresh sage leaves
- 2 pounds (910 g) octopus, cleaned, tentacles cut into 3 pieces, and heads halved
- 1½ pounds (680 g) cuttlefish, cleaned
- 2½ cups (625 g) passata or tomato puree
- 1 pound (455 g) monkfish, cut into 3-inch (7.5 cm) pieces
- 1 pound (455 g) shrimp, heads on if possible
- 2 pounds (910 g) mussels
- Salt
- 1 loaf semolina bread, sliced

1. In a large skillet with a lid, heat the olive oil over medium-high heat. Add 8 of the garlic cloves, the red pepper flakes, and the sage. Cook, stirring occasionally, for 1 minute. Add the octopus and cook, tossing with a wooden spoon until the purple liquid is drawn out, 3 to 5 minutes. Reduce the heat to low, cover the pan, and simmer until the octopus is tender, 40 to 45 minutes. Check on the octopus occasionally; if it looks dry, add a few tablespoons of water.
2. Add the cuttlefish and cook, tossing with a wooden spoon, for 1 minute. Add the passata and 1 cup (240 ml) of water. Increase the heat to medium-high and bring the mixture to a boil. Reduce the heat to low, cover the pan, and simmer until the sauce reduces a bit, about 20 minutes. Add the monkfish, cover, and cook for 20 minutes. Add the shrimp and mussels. Increase the heat to medium-high and cook until the shrimp are firm and the mussels open, 10 to 15 minutes. Discard any mussels that have not opened. Season with salt to taste. Let rest for 15 minutes before serving.
3. Meanwhile, toast the garlic bread: Preheat the oven to 400°F (200°C).
4. Rub each slice of bread with the remaining garlic clove and drizzle with olive oil. Arrange the slices in a single layer on a baking sheet and bake until golden, about 10 minutes.
5. Ladle the stew into bowls and serve with the bread.

Nonna Romana Sciddurlo's

VONGOLE GRATINATE

BAKED CLAMS

Prep time: 15 minutes
Cook time: 10 minutes
Yield: 12 servings

On Christmas Eve, there never seems to be enough baked clams, and a good baked clam is a thing of beauty. You will find them on most Italian-American restaurant menus, and everyone—and I do mean everyone—has their own secret to the bread-crumb topping, which can make or break this dish. Nonna Romana's secret is to keep it incredibly simple. She says no to crazy spices and wine, which can overpower the delicate flavor of the clams. But she says a resounding yes to a bit of Pecorino Romano, which is the only cheese she dares mix with any shellfish (but never on a pasta dish). Make sure to use a smaller variety of clams, which are more flavorful; littlenecks are ideal.

24 littleneck clams, scrubbed
1 cup (115 g) plain bread crumbs
1 tablespoon grated Pecorino Romano cheese
4 cloves garlic, minced
2 tablespoons minced fresh parsley
¼ cup (60 ml) extra-virgin olive oil, plus more for drizzling
¼ teaspoon salt
Dash black pepper
Lemon wedges, for serving

1. Preheat the oven to 500°F (250°C).
2. Shuck the clams with a bowl underneath to catch the juice and leave the meat on the half shell. Reserve the juice from the clams. Alternatively, heat a medium stockpot with a lid over medium heat and add the clams. Cover and cook just until the clams begin to open, about 2 minutes. (You don't want to cook them, just open the shells.) Using a shucking knife, pry open the shells and position the meat on the half shell. Place the clams on a baking sheet.
3. In a medium bowl, stir together the bread crumbs, cheese, garlic, parsley, and olive oil until the mixture looks uniformly wet. Season with the salt and pepper to taste.
4. Cover each clam with 1 heaping tablespoon of the bread-crumb mixture. Do not pack it down. Drizzle the clams with olive oil. Pour the reserved clam juice into the bottom of the baking sheet.
5. Bake for 5 to 7 minutes. Turn the oven to broil and broil the clams for 1 minute to brown, watching closely to prevent burning. Serve with the lemon wedges.

Nonna Rosa Carmelo's

CALAMARI ALLA GRAFFIU

BAKED CALAMARI WITH BREAD CRUMBS

Prep time: 15 minutes
Cook time: 18 minutes
Yield: 4 to 6 servings

My Zia Rosa may kill me for letting you guys in on this little secret, but I have to tell the truth: This particular recipe actually belongs to my Zio Domenico. Variations of this super-simple baked calamari dish, known as *calamari alla graffiu* in Puglia, can be found throughout southern Italy. My Zio Domenico spent nearly half a century working at the Italian-American institution that is Gargiulo's restaurant in Coney Island, and in between waiting tables, he wandered into the kitchen to learn a few things. One day years ago, he came home and tried to replicate their famous baked calamari, which are tossed in a delicious savory bread crumb and cheese mixture that becomes beautifully charred in a hot oven. The secret is giving the pan a good scrape every few minutes, so they char evenly on all sides.

- 2 pounds (910 g) cleaned calamari, bodies cut into 1½-inch (4 cm) rings and tentacles left whole
- 1 cup (240 ml) extra-virgin olive oil
- 2 cups (230 g) plain bread crumbs
- ¾ cup (75 g) grated Pecorino Romano cheese
- ¼ cup (15 g) minced fresh parsley
- 10 cloves garlic, minced
- ½ teaspoon salt
- ¼ teaspoon black pepper
- Lemon wedges, for serving

1. Preheat the oven to 500°F (250°C).
2. Rinse the calamari under cold running water and pat dry with a paper towel. Make sure the calamari are as dry as possible.
3. Place the olive oil in a small bowl.
4. In a medium bowl, combine the bread crumbs, cheese, parsley, garlic, salt, and pepper.
5. Dip the calamari in the oil and then in the bread crumb mixture. Shake off the excess and spread the calamari onto 2 baking sheets, making sure not to overcrowd them.
6. Bake until the calamari are very golden brown and almost charred, 15 to 18 minutes. Using a metal spatula, scrape and turn the calamari halfway through the baking time. Serve with the lemon wedges.

Nonna Antoinette Capodicci's

PIZZE FRITTE CON BACCALÀ E ACCIUGHE

FRITTERS WITH BACCALÀ AND ANCHOVIES

Prep time: 2 hours 30 minutes, plus 1 to 3 days soaking

Cook time: 30 minutes

Yield: About 60 fritters

1 pound (455 g) baccalà (salt cod)
½ teaspoon sugar
2 cups (480 ml) warm water, divided
1 packet (¼ ounce/7 g) active dry yeast
4 cups (480 g) all-purpose or 00 flour
2 teaspoons salt
1 teaspoon black pepper
Oil-packed anchovy fillets, as desired, broken into small pieces
Oil, for frying

"On Christmas we gotta have the *pizze fritt' e baccalà*," Nonna Antoinette says to me. Even when she speaks English, it's with a little Neapolitan flair! Pizze fritte are a classic savory variety of *zeppole* from the Naples area that are filled with steamed baccalà or salty anchovies and fried to perfection.

1. Put the baccalà in a large bowl with enough cold water to cover it. Place the bowl in the refrigerator and change the water 3 times a day; repeat for 1 to 3 days, depending on saltiness. Drain.
2. In a small stockpot, add the baccalà and enough cold water to cover it; bring to a boil over high heat. Reduce the heat to a simmer and cook until the baccalà flakes easily, 15 to 20 minutes. Transfer to a plate and set aside until cool enough to handle, then shred it by hand into small pieces.
3. In a small bowl, dissolve the sugar in 1 cup (240 ml) of the warm water. Add the yeast and let sit until the mixture begins to bubble, 3 to 5 minutes.
4. In a large bowl, combine the flour, salt, and pepper. Whisk in the yeast mixture and the remaining 1 cup (240 ml) warm water until a very soft batter forms. Continue whisking until the mixture is very smooth, 3 to 5 minutes. Cover the bowl with plastic wrap and set aside in a very warm place until the batter doubles in size, about 2 hours.
5. Take a full tablespoon of dough and stuff it with pieces of baccalà or bits of anchovy as desired, making sure it's fully enclosed. Repeat with the remaining dough, baccalà, and anchovy as desired.
6. Line a plate with paper towels. In a small stockpot, heat about 2 inches (5 cm) of oil over high heat.
7. Working in batches, carefully drop the filled dough into the hot oil and fry until golden, 2 to 3 minutes per batch. Transfer to the prepared plate. Serve hot.

Nonna Rina Pesce's

LINGUINE CON CAPITONE

LINGUINE WITH EEL

Prep time: 2 hours
Cook time: 45 minutes
Yield: 4 to 6 servings

Of all the dishes served on *la Vigilia*, eel has the longest-standing place in Italian Christmas tradition. I still know many families who make their way to remote fish stores, hours away, to purchase an eel and let it live rent-free in their bathtub until Christmas Eve. The tradition of eating *capitone*, a female eel, has been going on for centuries in southern Italy, and is rooted deep in superstition. It is said that the eel symbolizes the snake that tempted Eve in the garden of Eden, and by eating it on Christmas Eve, it is possible to conquer it and ward off evil spirits. Most families who still carry on the tradition prefer to have their fishmonger clean and skin the eel for them, and I recommend doing the same.

- 1½ pounds (680 g) fresh eel, cut into 3- to 4-inch-long (7.5 to 10 cm) pieces
- ½ cup (120 ml) red wine vinegar
- 2 tablespoons extra-virgin olive oil
- 4 cloves garlic
- 4 bay leaves
- ½ cup (120 ml) dry white wine, such as Pinot Grigio
- 1 can (14 ounces/400 g) crushed tomatoes
- ¼ teaspoon red pepper flakes
- 2 tablespoons minced fresh parsley, divided
- Salt
- 16 ounces (455 g) dried linguine

1. In a large bowl, add the eel pieces and enough cold running water to cover them. Add the vinegar and soak for 2 hours. Drain and rinse the eel under cold running water.
2. In a large skillet with a lid, heat the olive oil over medium heat. Add the garlic and bay leaves; cook, stirring occasionally, until the garlic has colored and is fragrant, 1 to 2 minutes. Add the eel and sear all over, 5 to 7 minutes. Add the wine and cook until the alcohol evaporates, about 2 minutes. Stir in the tomatoes, red pepper flakes, 1 tablespoon of the parsley, and 1½ cups (360 ml) of water. Reduce the heat to low, cover the pan, and simmer for 30 minutes. Season with salt to taste.
3. Bring a medium stockpot of generously salted water to a boil over high heat. Drop in the linguine. Cook 1 to 2 minutes shy of al dente. Drain the pasta and add it to the sauce along with the remaining 1 tablespoon parsley. Cook, tossing, for 1 to 2 minutes over medium-high heat. Serve immediately in warm bowls.

Nonna Rosa Carmelo's

ZUPPA DI COZZE CON POMODORO

MUSSELS IN RED SAUCE

Prep time: 10 minutes
Cook time: 20 minutes
Yield: 6 servings

Mussels were always plentiful and inexpensive in southern Italy, especially in Puglia, where my family has roots. Back in Italy, my Zia Rosa would have classically prepared these in *bianco*, in a simple white wine sauce. She learned to make them in this delightfully spicy red sauce from a Neapolitan neighbor in Brooklyn. We look forward to them every Christmas Eve, with crusty bread for dipping!

¼ cup (60 ml) extra-virgin olive oil, divided
6 cloves garlic, divided
2 pounds (910 g) mussels, scrubbed and debearded
½ cup (120 ml) white wine
2 tablespoons minced fresh parsley, divided
¼ teaspoon red pepper flakes, or to taste
1 can (14 ounces/400 g) crushed tomatoes
Salt
Italian bread, for serving (optional)

1. Line a fine-mesh strainer with a piece of cheesecloth. Heat a small stockpot over medium heat and add 2 tablespoons of the olive oil. Once hot, add 3 of the garlic cloves. Cook, stirring occasionally, until golden and fragrant, about 2 minutes. Add the mussels and cover the pot. Cook, stirring, until the mussels partially open, 2 to 3 minutes.
2. Add the wine and 1 tablespoon of the parsley; cook, stirring occasionally, until the alcohol evaporates and the mussels fully open. Discard any mussels that have not opened and transfer the rest to a large bowl. Strain the mussel broth through the prepared strainer.
3. In a large skillet, heat the remaining 2 tablespoons olive oil over medium-high heat. Add the red pepper flakes and the remaining 3 garlic cloves; cook, stirring occasionally, until the garlic is golden, 1 to 2 minutes. Stir in the crushed tomatoes and remaining 1 tablespoon parsley; cook, stirring occasionally, for about 5 minutes. Stir in the strained mussel broth and bring to a boil over medium-high heat; cook for 3 to 4 minutes. Season with salt to taste. Add the mussels, cover the pan, and cook for 4 to 5 minutes.
4. Serve with crusty Italian bread, if desired.

Nonna Maria Fiore's

PETTOLE CON OLIVE

FRITTERS WITH BLACK OLIVES

Prep time: 1 hour
Cook time: 20 minutes
Yield: About 48 fritters

Pettole are a type of yeast *zeppole* from southern Italy, usually eaten on Christmas Eve. Many villages also have pettole recipes that correspond with different saint days and holidays. Nonna Maria's pettole, with salt-cured olives, are a savory treat that works beautifully as an appetizer or even as a great addition to a holiday bread basket.

1¼ cups (150 g) all-purpose or 00 flour
1 teaspoon salt
1 packet (¼ ounce/7 g) active dry yeast
1 cup (240 ml) warm water
2 large eggs, at room temperature
1 cup (155 g) salt-cured olives, pitted and finely chopped
Olive oil, for dipping and frying

1. In a small bowl, whisk together the flour and salt.
2. In a large bowl, dissolve the yeast in the warm water and set aside until it bubbles, about 3 minutes. Stir in the eggs until incorporated. Little by little, add the flour-salt mixture, stirring until fully incorporated and a smooth dough forms. Fold in the olives. Cover the bowl with plastic wrap and set aside in a warm place until the dough doubles in size, 45 minutes to 1 hour.
3. Line a plate with paper towels. In a small stockpot, heat about 1½ inches (4 cm) of olive oil over high heat.
4. Fill a cup with some olive oil and have the risen dough handy. Dip a small ice cream scoop into the olive oil, then scoop a piece of the dough. Working in batches, carefully drop the dough into the hot oil. Fry the fritters until golden brown, about 2 minutes per batch. Transfer to the paper towel-lined plate. Serve hot or warm.

Nonna Romana Sciddurlo's

MERLUZZI FRITTI

FRIED WHITING

Prep time: 4 hours 20 minutes

Cook time: 25 minutes

Yield: 8 to 10 servings

Whiting, or *merluzzi*, is a small fish that is often fried whole and then marinated in garlic, mint, and vinegar. While this dish can be a bit of an acquired taste, you just have to have some fried whiting for a proper old-school Italian Christmas Eve. Nonna Romana and her sisters used to chase me around the house on Christmas Eve with a big plate trying to get me to eat it because the fish is considered "brain food," but today, I don't need too much convincing. I love how this fish is cooked with all the bones in, making its flesh super succulent.

WHITING

2 pounds (910 g) whiting, cleaned and gutted

All-purpose or 00 flour, for dredging

Olive oil, for frying

VINAIGRETTE MARINADE

2 tablespoons minced fresh mint

5 cloves garlic, minced

½ cup (120 ml) red wine vinegar

1. **To make the whiting:** Rinse the whiting under cold running water and pat dry with paper towels. Get the fish as dry as possible to prevent the flour from caking on it.
2. Line a plate with paper towels and place the flour in a shallow bowl.
3. Heat about 1½ inches (4 cm) of olive oil in a medium skillet over high heat. Dredge each whiting in the flour. Carefully add 2 or 3 pieces at a time to the hot oil and fry until golden brown, 4 to 5 minutes per batch. Transfer to the prepared plate. Let cool to room temperature.
4. **To make the vinaigrette marinade:** In a small bowl, whisk together the mint, garlic, and vinegar.
5. In a 9 by 13-inch (23 by 33 cm) baking dish, arrange the fried whiting in a single layer. Drizzle the marinade over the fish and refrigerate for at least 4 hours or up to overnight. This can be made up to 2 days in advance.

Nonna Maria Pesce's

GAMBERI AL FORNO

BAKED SHRIMP WITH BREAD CRUMBS

Prep time: 5 minutes
Cook time: 30 minutes
Yield: 6 to 8 servings

This shrimp recipe is fast, easy, and super flavorful. Nonna Maria usually has the shrimp ready to go on a baking sheet and pops them in the oven as soon as guests arrive, so they're cooked to perfection by the time everyone is ready to eat. They're great for holiday entertaining because they can be served hot, but they're just as delicious at room temperature.

½ cup (120 ml) extra-virgin olive oil, plus more for greasing and drizzling

2 tablespoons minced fresh parsley

1 teaspoon dried oregano

¼ cup (30 g) plain bread crumbs

¼ cup (25 g) grated Pecorino Romano cheese

Salt and black pepper

2 pounds (910 g) jumbo shrimp, peeled and deveined, tails on

1. Preheat the oven to 370°F (188°C). Grease a baking sheet with olive oil.
2. In a medium bowl, combine the parsley, oregano, bread crumbs, cheese, and salt and pepper to taste.
3. In a large bowl, toss the shrimp with the olive oil, until the shrimp are evenly coated. Add the bread crumb mixture and toss until evenly coated. Arrange the shrimp on the prepared baking sheet and drizzle with a bit more olive oil.
4. Bake until the shrimp are golden, about 30 minutes. For a bit more color, broil for 1 to 2 minutes, if desired.

Nonna Teresa Petruccelli-Formato's

PICCIALETIEGLI

SAVORY FRITTERS WITH CINNAMON AND CLOVES

Prep time: 1 hour 15 minutes
Cook time: 15 minutes
Yield: About 12 fritters

The shape of *piccialatiegli* resembles a pretzel, and once the dough hits the hot oil, its unmistakable aroma fills Nonna Teresa's kitchen in Queens, New York. She adopted her Neapolitan mother-in-law's tradition of making these savory fritters on Christmas Eve. "When my mother-in-law was alive, she would be rolling the dough and someone else would fry them, and we could never make enough because everyone would eat them as we made them. She would always want to drop the last one into the oil herself, and she would proudly declare, '*E quest' é cento!* (And this makes one hundred!)'"

3 cups (360 g) all-purpose or 00 flour, plus more for dusting
1 teaspoon ground cinnamon
1 teaspoon salt
1 teaspoon ground cloves
½ teaspoon ground nutmeg
1 teaspoon sugar
1¼ cups (300 ml) warm water
1 packet (¼ ounce/7 g) active dry yeast
1 tablespoon extra-virgin olive oil
Oil, for frying

1. In a medium bowl, whisk together the flour, cinnamon, salt, cloves, and nutmeg.
2. In the bowl of a stand mixer fritted with the dough hook attachment, dissolve the sugar in the warm water. Add the yeast and let sit until the mixture begins to bubble, 3 to 5 minutes. Add the olive oil. With the mixer running at low speed, gradually add the dry ingredients to the wet ingredients. Increase the speed to medium and mix until a sticky dough begins to form, about 3 minutes. Cover the bowl with plastic wrap and set aside in a warm place to rise for about 1 hour (see Nonna Teresa Says).
3. Lightly flour a work surface and turn the dough out onto it. Knead the dough for 5 minutes, then divide it into 12 or 13 equal pieces. Flour your hands and roll each piece into ropes, 10 to 12 inches (25 to 30 cm) long and 2 inches (5 cm) thick. Cross one end of dough over the other to create a fish or cross shape.
4. In a small heavy-bottomed stockpot, heat about 3 inches (7.5 cm) of oil over high heat. Working in batches of 2 or 3 at a time, carefully drop the dough into the hot oil and fry until brown, about 2 minutes per batch. Serve immediately.

Nonna Teresa Says

If you cannot find a warm spot in the house to let the dough rise, place the bowl inside your oven with the light on. The oven should be a constant 80 to 85°F (27 to 30°C)—the perfect environment to let dough rise.

Nonna Romana Sciddurlo's

CALAMARI FRITTI

FRIED CALAMARI

Prep time: 15 minutes
Cook time: 20 minutes
Yield: 4 to 6 servings

Fried calamari hits everyone's Italian comfort-food spot. The plate never makes it more than one round around the dinner table! Nonna Romana's calamari are coated in refined semolina flour, which gives them a little more texture and a gorgeous golden color. In Italy, fried calamari aren't quite as crunchy as they are here in the States. The outside coating is light and delicate, and doesn't overpower the seafood. These can be served Italian-American style with marinara sauce, but my favorite is simply with a squeeze of fresh lemon.

2 cups (334 g) refined semolina flour

2 tablespoons salt, plus more for sprinkling

2 pounds (910 g) cleaned calamari, bodies cut into ½-inch (13 mm) rings and tentacles left whole

Oil, for frying

1. In a large mixing bowl, whisk together the semolina and salt, breaking up any lumps.
2. With a paper towel, pat the calamari dry. Get them as dry as possible or else they will be soggy.
3. Line a plate with paper towels. Heat about 2 inches (5 cm) of oil in a large heavy-bottomed skillet over high heat.
4. Dredge the calamari in the semolina mixture and transfer to a fine-mesh strainer to shake off any excess. Make sure all the pieces have an even coating. Working in 5 or 6 batches, place the calamari in the oil and fry until lightly golden brown, 3 to 4 minutes per batch. Transfer to the prepared plate. Sprinkle with extra salt. Serve immediately.

Nonna Romana Says

Calamari need room! Don't overcrowd the pan when you're frying, or the calamari won't brown.

Nonna Romana Sciddurlo's

CALAMARI RIPIENI CON SPAGHETTI

STUFFED CALAMARI WITH SPAGHETTI

Prep time: 15 minutes
Cook time: 55 minutes
Yield: 4 to 6 servings

Helping Nonna Romana stuff calamari brings back so many memories from my childhood. She would ask me to help her because my little fingers were best for getting all the stuffing inside the calamari tube. Today, we still do it together but with demitasse spoons instead. We then cook them in a slightly spicy tomato sauce and say a prayer that the filling doesn't come out as the calamari shrink.

SAUCE

3 tablespoons extra-virgin olive oil

1 small onion, cut into ¼-inch (6 mm) dice

42 ounces (1.25 L) crushed tomatoes

2 tablespoons chopped fresh parsley

Pinch salt

¼ teaspoon red pepper flakes

CALAMARI

2 large eggs

¾ cup (75 g) grated Pecorino Romano cheese

⅓ cup (38 g) plain bread crumbs

3 tablespoons extra-virgin olive oil

2 tablespoons chopped fresh parsley

3 cloves garlic, finely chopped

Salt and black pepper

1 to 2 tablespoons milk, as needed

1 pound (455 g) cleaned whole fresh calamari

16 ounces (455 g) dried spaghetti

1. **To make the sauce:** In a large skillet, heat the olive oil over medium heat. Add the onion and cook, stirring occasionally, until translucent, 3 to 5 minutes. Stir in the tomatoes, parsley, salt, and red pepper flakes and bring the sauce to a boil, then reduce the heat to low. Simmer for 15 to 20 minutes.
2. **To make the calamari:** In a medium bowl, stir together the eggs, Pecorino Romano, bread crumbs, olive oil, parsley, and garlic. Season with salt and pepper. Mix well until a semisoft stuffing forms. If the mixture looks dry, add 1 to 2 tablespoons of milk as needed.
3. Using a teaspoon, fill the bodies of the calamari with the stuffing up to ½ inch (12 mm) from the top. Be careful not to overfill. Secure the calamari with toothpicks, if necessary. (The calamari will shrink as they cook, so it's normal to have some filling come out.)
4. Add the calamari to the sauce and cover the pan. Continue to cook over low heat for 25 to 30 minutes. From time to time, stir the sauce and the calamari to prevent them from sticking to the bottom. Transfer the calamari and sauce to a rimmed serving dish.
5. Bring a medium stockpot of generously salted water to a boil over high heat. Drop in the spaghetti. Cook until al dente. Add the spaghetti to the sauce and toss for 1 to 2 minutes over medium heat. Serve the spaghetti in bowls, topped with the stuffed calamari.

Nonna Romana Sciddurlo's

LINGUINE ALLE VONGOLE

LINGUINE IN WHITE CLAM SAUCE

Prep time: 10 minutes

Cook time: 20 minutes

Yield: 4 to 6 servings

Okay, so I have a confession to make: Nonna Romana learned this recipe from my dad, Vito! In our family, he is undoubtedly the king of the clam sauce, and it's so good, we usually demand he make it for nearly every holiday. Over the years, Nonna has battled with him over who makes it best, and while her original clam sauce was quite good, the version she makes today is more my father's. The secret to a good white clam sauce, which is more popular in Italy than the red variety, lies in its simplicity. The fewer ingredients, the better, and you must always—always!—use fresh clams. For this dish, you will want to use the smallest clams possible, which pack in a lot more flavor, so if you can find cockles, use them.

36 littleneck clams or 3 pounds (1.4 kg) cockles, scrubbed and rinsed

Salt

16 ounces (455 g) dried linguine

¼ cup (60 ml) extra-virgin olive oil

5 cloves garlic

¼ teaspoon red pepper flakes

2 tablespoons chopped fresh parsley, divided

½ cup (120 ml) dry white wine, such as Pinot Grigio

1. Heat a large saucepan with a lid over high heat and add the clams. Cover the pan and cook until the clams open completely, 5 to 7 minutes. Discard any clams that have not opened. Separate the meat from the shells and transfer to a medium bowl; discard most of the shells (reserve a few for garnish if you like). Strain the clam broth through a fine-mesh strainer lined with cheesecloth into a glass and rinse out the pan.
2. Bring a medium stockpot of generously salted water to a boil over high heat. Drop the linguine into the water.
3. In the rinsed saucepan, heat the olive oil over medium heat. Add the garlic and red pepper flakes and cook, stirring occasionally, for 1 minute. Add the strained clam broth and 1 tablespoon of the parsley. Bring to a boil, add the wine, and cook, stirring occasionally, until the alcohol evaporates, 2 to 3 minutes. Add the shelled clams; cook for 3 to 4 minutes.
4. Scoop out 1 cup (240 ml) of the pasta cooking water. Once the pasta is just shy of al dente, scoop it out and add it to the pan with the clams. Cook, tossing, for 1 to 2 minutes. If the pasta looks a bit dry, add some of the reserved pasta cooking water. Sprinkle with the remaining 1 tablespoon parsley and serve immediately.

CHRISTMAS DAY

Nonna Antoinette Capodicci's

SARTÙ DI RISO

RICE TIMBALLO

Prep time: 20 minutes
Cook time: 2 hour 30 minutes
Yield: 10 servings

When Nonna Antoinette wants to make something super special that will impress her holiday guests, she makes her famous *sartù di riso alla Napoletana*. The first time I ever saw a sartù, I was completely mesmerized. Nonna Antoinette makes a mold of meat sauce–flavored rice in a Bundt pan and fills it with sautéed peas, pancetta, and hard-boiled eggs. And did I mention tiny meatballs?

SAUCE

¼ cup (60 ml) extra-virgin olive oil

1 small onion, cut into ¼-inch (6 mm) dice

1 clove garlic, cut into ¼-inch (6 mm) dice

6 ounces (170 g) sweet Italian sausage links (2 or 3 links)

2 cans (28 ounces/794 g each) crushed tomatoes

Salt

4 fresh basil leaves

MEATBALLS

1 slice day-old Italian bread, crust removed

¼ cup (60 ml) whole milk

1 large egg, beaten

½ teaspoon salt

¼ teaspoon black pepper

⅛ teaspoon garlic powder

¼ cup (25 g) grated Parmigiano-Reggiano cheese

¼ pound (113 g) ground beef

Olive oil, for frying

1. **To make the sauce:** In a small stockpot, heat the olive oil over medium-high heat. Add the onion, garlic, and sausage and cook, stirring frequently, until the sausage has browned and the onion is soft, 7 to 10 minutes. Stir in the crushed tomatoes, 1 cup (240 ml) of water, and salt to taste. Reduce the heat to low, cover the pan, and simmer until the sauce thickens and is slightly reduced, about 1 hour.
2. Remove from the heat and stir in the basil. Remove the sausage from the sauce and slice the links into ¼-inch-thick (6 mm) slices. Transfer to a plate. Set the sauce aside, uncovered.
3. **To make the meatballs:** In a small bowl, combine the bread and milk. Let sit for 2 to 3 minutes.
4. In a medium bowl, combine the egg, salt, pepper, garlic powder, cheese, and ground beef. Squeeze the excess moisture out of the bread and add it to the meat mixture. Mix with your hands until well combined. With damp hands, roll the mixture into ½-inch (12 mm) balls.
5. Line a plate with paper towels. In a medium heavy-bottomed skillet, heat about 1 inch (2.5 cm) of olive oil over high heat. Working in batches, fry the meatballs until browned on all sides, about 2 minutes per batch. Transfer to the prepared plate.
6. **To make the rice:** In a small stockpot, bring 3 quarts (2.8 L) of water and the salt to a boil over high heat. Add the rice and cook until al dente, 20 to 25 minutes. Drain and transfer to a medium bowl.

CONTINUED ON PAGE 134

CONTINUED FROM PAGE 133

RICE

2 teaspoons salt

16 ounces (455 g) Arborio rice, rinsed

3 large eggs, beaten

2 cups (200 g) grated Parmigiano-Reggiano cheese

PEAS

2 tablespoons extra-virgin olive oil

½ small onion, cut into ¼-inch (6 mm) dice

2 ounces (55 g) pancetta, cut into ¼-inch (6 mm) dice

1 cup (130 g) frozen peas, thawed

1 ounce (28 g) dried porcini mushrooms, rehydrated and finely chopped (optional)

ASSEMBLY

2 tablespoons (30 g) unsalted butter, at room temperature, divided

¼ cup (30 g) plain bread crumbs

2 large hard-cooked eggs, peeled and cut into small chunks

8 ounces (225 g) fresh mozzarella cheese, cut into ½-inch (13 mm) dice

¼ cup (25 g) grated Parmigiano-Reggiano cheese, divided

7 Stir 2 cups (480 ml) of the sauce into the rice. On a baking sheet, spread the rice in an even layer and let cool for 10 to 15 minutes. When cool, return the rice to the bowl and mix in the beaten eggs and Parmigiano-Reggiano.

8 **To make the peas:** Heat a small skillet over medium-high heat. Add the olive oil, onion, and pancetta and cook, stirring occasionally, until the pancetta is crisp and the onion is soft, 3 to 5 minutes. Add the peas and cook, stirring frequently, for 5 minutes. If using, add the rehydrated porcinis and cook, stirring occasionally, for 2 to 3 minutes. Remove from the heat and set aside.

9 **To assemble:** Preheat the oven to 350°F (180°C). Grease a 12-cup (2.8 L) Bundt pan with 1 tablespoon of the butter. Coat the pan evenly with bread crumbs, making sure there are no bare spots. Press half of the rice mixture into the bottom of the pan. Wet your hands and press the rice firmly to coat the bottom and all the way up the sides and middle of the pan. Use the back of a wet spoon to make a well in the rice. Fill the well with the sliced sausage, meatballs, peas, hard-boiled egg pieces, and mozzarella, and evenly pack down the filling. Top with 2 tablespoons of sauce, 2 tablespoons of the Parmigiano-Reggiano, and the remaining rice. Wet your hands and firmly pack down the rice. Top with 2 tablespoons of sauce and sprinkle with the remaining 2 tablespoons Parmigiano-Reggiano. Dot the top with the remaining 1 tablespoon butter.

10 Bake for 40 to 45 minutes. Let rest for 15 to 20 minutes before inverting and cutting. To invert, wearing oven mitts, place a large plate over the bottom of the Bundt pan. Place one hand over the top of the pan and flip the pan over onto the plate. Place the plate on the counter and lift the pan off. Serve warm.

If you don't love some of the filling ingredients, feel free to leave them out.

Nonna Maria Fiore's Nonna Maria's

POLPETTE DI ZUCCHINE

ZUCCHINI FRITTERS

Prep time: 5 minutes

Cook time: 12 minutes

Yield: About 24 fritters

1 medium zucchini, finely minced

1 small onion, minced

6 tablespoons grated Pecorino Romano cheese

2 tablespoons plain bread crumbs

2 tablespoons minced fresh parsley

3 large eggs

2 tablespoons all-purpose or 00 flour

1 teaspoon salt

¼ teaspoon black pepper

Oil, for frying

Try as you might, it is simply impossible to have just one of Nonna Maria's zucchini fritters. She mixes finely chopped zucchini into a thick batter and fries them until they're golden brown and irresistible, making them the perfect holiday finger food.

1. In a medium bowl, combine the zucchini, onion, cheese, bread crumbs, parsley, eggs, flour, salt, and pepper. The batter should be thick enough to drop by the spoonful.
2. Line a plate with paper towels. In a medium skillet, heat about 1½ inches (4 cm) of oil over medium-high heat. Working in batches, drop tablespoons of the batter into the hot oil. Fry until the fritters are golden brown, about 2 minutes per batch. Transfer to the prepared plate. Serve hot.

Nonna Annita Fallone Apruzzese's

STRACCIATELLA

EGG DROP CHICKEN SOUP

Prep time: 15 minutes
Cook time: 2 hours
Yield: 4 to 6 servings

Stracciatella is one of those things that is so super simple to make that you would wonder why you even need a recipe. Nonna Annita has been making this soup since her childhood in Lazio's Ciociaria and swears that the mastery of this iconic Italian egg drop soup is a combination of technique and high-quality ingredients. Sure, you can use store-bought chicken stock, but her homemade recipe really takes it to the next level. In her home, this is the perfect Christmas Day first course that doesn't fill her guests up too much.

- 4 quarts (3.8 L) cold water
- 2 teaspoons salt, plus more to taste
- 2 ribs celery, ends trimmed
- 10 baby carrots
- ½ whole chicken or 2 pounds (910 g) bone-in chicken thighs, rinsed under cold running water
- Black pepper
- 3 large eggs

1. In a small stockpot, bring the cold water, salt, celery, and carrots to a boil over high heat. Add the chicken and reduce the heat to low. Cover the pot halfway and simmer for 1 hour and 30 minutes.
2. Remove from the heat and transfer the chicken and vegetables to a bowl. Set aside until cool enough to handle. Reserve the meat for a different use. Discard the vegetables.
3. Using a fine-mesh strainer, strain the broth into another pot. Bring to a boil over high heat. Season with more salt and pepper to taste. Reduce the heat to low.
4. Crack the eggs, one at a time, into a small bowl and beat. Using a fork, stir the broth in a circular motion while drizzling the eggs into the moving broth. Stir the eggs gently with the fork until strings form, about 1 minute. Bring to a boil once more and serve immediately.

Nonna Dorotea Cristino's

COSTATA DI MANZO

RIB-EYE ROAST

Prep time: 18 minutes

Cook time: 4 hours

Yield: 6 to 8 servings

A good rib-eye roast is a safe bet to serve for any holiday. Nonna Dorotea's secret to a good roast is inserting whole garlic cloves into the meat as it cooks, so it absorbs the garlic's amazing flavor. If you're reading this recipe and think it sounds like a lot of garlic, it is, but Nonna knows best!

SPICE RUB

¼ cup (34 g) minced garlic (about 10 cloves)

3 tablespoons Italian seasoning

3 tablespoons coarse kosher salt

3 tablespoons whole black peppercorns

½ cup (120 ml) extra-virgin olive oil

ROAST

1 boneless beef rib eye (7 pounds/3.2 kg), not trimmed

30 cloves garlic

1. Preheat the oven to 400°F (200°C).
2. **To make the spice rub:** In a small bowl, stir together the garlic, Italian seasoning, salt, peppercorns, and olive oil.
3. **To make the roast:** Using a sharp knife, make 30 cuts all over the roast, about 2 inches (5 cm) deep. Insert 1 whole garlic clove into each cut. If a clove is too large, cut it in half. Rub the spice rub all over the roast, coating the entire surface. Massage the rub into the roast for 2 to 3 minutes. On the rack of a large roasting pan, place the roast, fatty side up. Roast for 30 minutes.
4. Adjust the oven control to 325°F (170°C) and roast until an instant-read meat thermometer reads 150°F (66°C) for medium-rare or 160°F (71°C) for medium, 3 hours and 30 minutes to 4 hours. Let the roast rest for 15 to 20 minutes.
5. Using a very sharp knife, cut the roast into 1-inch-thick (2.5 cm) slices. Strain the juices from the pan through a fine-mesh strainer and serve with the roast.

Nonna Rina Mulazzi's

CAPPELLETTI IN BRODO

LITTLE HATS FILLED WITH CHEESE AND MORTADELLA IN BROTH

Prep time: 1 hour 30 minutes
Cook time: 1 hour 35 minutes
Yield: 4 to 6 servings

At Nonna Rina's house, Christmas is a big event and warrants a very special fresh pasta from her beloved Emilia Romagna. Watching her skilled hands roll out the dough into paper-thin sheets is a thing of absolute magic. This step can be a bit tricky, so don't feel bad if you need to use the stand mixer. The word *cappelletti* in Italian means "little hats," and Nonna Rina fills hers with a delicious mix of mortadella, ricotta, and stracchino cheese, which is a young and super creamy cow's milk cheese, typical of northern Italy. If stracchino is hard to find, substitute it with more ricotta.

BROTH

1 pound (455 g) bone-in chicken thighs
1½ pounds (680 g) bone-in beef short ribs
2 small carrots, cut into large chunks
2 ribs celery, cut into large chunks
1 Roma tomato, halved
1 small onion, halved
4 quarts (3.8 L) cold water
Salt and black pepper

FILLING

6 ounces (170 g) mortadella
¾ cup (185 g) ricotta impastata
6 ounces (170 g) stracchino cheese
9 tablespoons grated Parmigiano-Reggiano cheese, plus more for serving
1 large egg yolk
Dash ground nutmeg

PASTA DOUGH

2½ cups (300 g) all-purpose or 00 flour
3 large eggs, at room temperature, well beaten
1 large egg yolk, at room temperature, well beaten
¼ teaspoon salt

1 **To make the broth:** In a small stockpot, add the chicken, short ribs, carrots, celery, tomato, onion, and cold water; bring to a boil over high heat. Skim off any foam that forms on top. Once you have removed all the foam and the pot is at a rolling boil, reduce the heat to low and simmer, uncovered, until reduced by one-fourth, 1 hour to 1 hour and 30 minutes.

2 Transfer the meat to a bowl. Remove and discard the vegetables. Let the meat cool and reserve it for another use. Strain the broth through a fine-mesh strainer into a large bowl. Season with salt and pepper as desired.

3 **To make the filling:** In a food processor fitted with the blade attachment, pulse the mortadella until coarsely chopped. Transfer to a medium bowl and add the ricotta, stracchino, Parmigiano-Reggiano, egg yolk, and nutmeg. Stir until smooth and fully incorporated.

4 **To make the pasta dough:** In the bowl of a stand mixer fitted with the dough hook attachment, add the flour, eggs, egg yolk, and salt; mix at low speed until the ingredients are incorporated and a dough forms, 5 to 6 minutes. Turn out the dough onto a clean work surface and knead with your hands, picking up any particles of dough as you go. If it feels dry, add 1 tablespoon of tepid water at a time until it comes together. Continue kneading until the dough is smooth and supple and has the consistency of play dough, 8 to 10 minutes. Wrap the dough ball in plastic wrap and let rest at room temperature for 30 minutes.

CONTINUED ON PAGE 140

CONTINUED FROM PAGE 138

5 Take one golf ball-size piece of dough at a time and roll it out with a rolling pin as thin as possible. Alternatively, use a pasta roller on a #3 setting and pass the dough through 2 or 3 times. Set the pasta roller to the #6 setting and roll out each piece of dough into sheets as thin as possible and you can almost see through them, 2 or 3 more times. Cover any sheets not being used with a clean, damp kitchen towel.

6 With a knife or a ravioli cutter, trim the dough sheets of any jagged ends into a clean square or rectangle. Cut out 2-inch (5 cm) squares. Place any scraps immediately under a damp kitchen towel so they do not dry out, and reroll.

7 Place 1 teaspoon of filling in the center of each square. Wet your finger with some water and dampen one corner. Close the square by folding one of the points over the filling to the opposite (wetted) point to create a little triangle. Wrap the pasta around your index finger so the two points of the triangle meet and overlap. Press them firmly together, making sure they are sealed. Transfer to a baking sheet, arranging the cappelletti in a single layer. Repeat with the remaining squares and filling. They can be cooked in the reserved broth immediately or frozen.

8 **To freeze:** Place the baking sheet in the freezer until the cappelletti are frozen. Store in resealable plastic bags in the freezer for up to 3 months. Do not thaw before cooking.

9 **To cook:** Bring the broth to a boil over medium-high heat. Drop the cappelletti into the boiling broth. Cook until they bob to the surface, 1 to 2 minutes. Serve with an extra sprinkle of grated Parmigiano-Reggiano cheese.

Nonna Rina Says

You must work with very small pieces of dough at a time or the pasta can dry out and crack.

Nonna Dorotea Cristino's

MANICOTTI CON RICOTTA E CARNE

RICOTTA AND MEAT-FILLED MANICOTTI

Prep time: 35 minutes

Cook time: 2 hour 30 minutes

Yield: About 24 crêpes; 8 to 10 servings

At Nonna Dorotea's house, there is never a unanimous decision on what kind of manicotti filling to make. "Nobody can make up their minds, so I always make both because I want to make everybody happy." Making two fillings might seem like a lot of work, but they're both a breeze, and the two trays of Italian comfort food will put a smile on everyone's face for your Christmas feast.

SAUCE

3 tablespoons extra-virgin olive oil

½ small onion, cut into ¼-inch (6 mm) dice

1 clove garlic, minced

2 cans (28 ounces/794 g) tomato puree

2 tablespoons minced fresh parsley

1½ teaspoons salt

Black pepper

CRÊPES

4 large eggs

2 cups (480 ml) whole milk

3 cups (360 g) all-purpose or 00 flour

Vegetable shortening, for cooking

RICOTTA FILLING

12 ounces (340 g) whole-milk ricotta

1 large egg

½ cup (50 g) grated Pecorino Romano cheese, plus more for sprinkling

1 cup (115 g) shredded fresh mozzarella cheese

1. **To make the sauce:** In a small stockpot with a lid, heat the olive oil over medium heat; add the onion and garlic and cook, stirring occasionally, until the garlic is golden and the onion is translucent, 5 to 7 minutes. Add the tomato puree and parsley. Fill each empty tomato puree can with 2 inches (5 cm) of water, swish them around, and add the tomato water to the pan. Add the salt and pepper and bring the sauce to a boil over medium-high heat. Reduce the heat to low, cover the pan, and simmer for 45 minutes to 1 hour. Uncover and let cool while you make the crêpes.
2. **To make the crêpes:** In a blender, process the eggs, milk, flour, and 1 cup (240 ml) of water until smooth, about 10 seconds. Transfer to a large bowl.
3. In a small nonstick skillet over low heat, melt ½ teaspoon of shortening. Add ¼ cup (60 ml) of batter to the pan and spread it in a circular motion with a fork. Cook until set in the middle, 1 to 2 minutes. Do not flip. Transfer to a baking sheet. Repeat with the remaining batter, adding a bit of shortening as needed to prevent sticking and arranging the cooked crêpes on baking sheets in a single layer until cool. Once cooled, the crêpes can be stacked and frozen in a resealable plastic bag for up to 3 months.
4. **To make the ricotta filling:** In a large bowl, combine the ricotta, egg, ¼ cup (60 ml) of the sauce, Pecorino Romano, and mozzarella. Mix well.
5. **To make the meat filling:** Heat a medium skillet over medium heat. Add the meat and cook, stirring occasionally, until well browned. Remove from the heat and stir in ¼ cup plus 2 tablespoons (90 ml) of the sauce, the Pecorino Romano, egg, salt, pepper, and mozzarella. Mix well.

CONTINUED ON PAGE 143

CONTINUED FROM PAGE 141

MEAT FILLING

¾ pound (340 g) ground sirloin

¼ cup (25 g) grated Pecorino Romano cheese

1 large egg

½ teaspoon salt

¼ teaspoon black pepper

¼ cup (29 g) shredded fresh mozzarella cheese

ASSEMBLY

2 tablespoons grated Pecorino Romano cheese

¼ cup (29 g) shredded fresh mozzarella cheese

6 **To assemble:** Preheat the oven to 380°F (193°C). In two 9 by 13-inch (23 by 33 cm) baking dishes, spread 1 cup (240 ml) of the sauce.

7 Fill half of the crêpes with 1½ tablespoons (23 g) of the ricotta filling; roll to close, and place, seam sides down, in a baking dish. Do not pack them too tightly. You should be able to fit 12 crêpes. Repeat with the remaining crêpes and the meat filling. Ladle about 1 cup (240 ml) of the sauce over the crêpes in each dish and sprinkle each with 1 tablespoon of the Pecorino Romano and 2 tablespoons of the mozzarella.

8 Cover the baking dishes with aluminum foil and bake until the cheese is bubbling, 25 to 30 minutes. Let rest for 15 minutes before serving.

Nonna Romana Sciddurlo's

LASAGNE CON POLPETTINE

LASAGNA WITH TINY MEATBALLS

Prep time: 30 minutes
Cook time: 1 hour 35 minutes
Yield: 6 to 8 servings

Nonna Romana's lasagna is her variation of a classic recipe from Puglia that uses a delicious sausage meat sauce and lots of little meatballs that I've helped roll every Christmas morning since I was a little girl. You can make and fry the meatballs the night before, but if you do, some of them may disappear.

SAUCE

3 tablespoons extra-virgin olive oil
3 cloves garlic, finely chopped
1 small onion, cut into ¼-inch (6 mm) dice
Red pepper flakes
1 pound (455 g) sweet Italian sausage
½ cup (120 ml) red wine, such as Merlot
2 cans (28 ounces/794 g) crushed tomatoes
1½ teaspoons salt
4 fresh basil leaves

MEATBALLS

1 pound (455 g) ground meatloaf mix (veal, pork, and beef)
2 large eggs
¾ cup (75 g) grated Pecorino Romano cheese
¾ cup (75 g) grated Parmigiano-Reggiano cheese
¾ cup (81 g) plain bread crumbs
3 tablespoons minced fresh parsley
2 cloves garlic, shaved
Oil, for frying

1 **To make the sauce:** In a large saucepan, heat the olive oil over medium heat. Add the garlic, onion, and red pepper flakes and cook, stirring occasionally, until the onion is soft, about 5 minutes. Add the sausage and cook, breaking up the sausage with a wooden spoon and stirring occasionally, until nicely browned, 5 to 7 minutes.

2 Add the wine and cook, stirring occasionally, until the alcohol evaporates, about 2 minutes. Stir in the tomatoes and salt. Fill each empty crushed tomato can about halfway with water and swish them around and add the tomato water. Tear the basil leaves and stir them in. Bring to a boil over high heat, then reduce the heat to low. Simmer for 20 to 30 minutes. Remove from the heat.

3 **To make the meatballs:** In a large bowl, combine the ground meat, eggs, Pecorino Romano, Parmigiano-Reggiano, bread crumbs, parsley, and garlic. Mix with your hands until well combined. Roll the mixture into ½-inch (12 mm) meatballs.

4 Line a plate with paper towels. In a large skillet, heat 1½ inches (4 cm) of oil over medium-high heat. Working in batches, fry the meatballs until golden brown, 1 to 2 minutes per batch. Transfer to the prepared plate.

5 **To make the lasagna:** Bring a large stockpot of generously salted water to a boil over high heat. Add the lasagna sheets and cook for about half the time listed on the package instructions. Drain and run the pasta sheets under cold running water. Lay the pasta sheets flat on a baking sheet or hang them over a colander.

LASAGNA

Salt

24 lasagna pasta sheets

16 ounces (455 g) fresh mozzarella cheese, shredded

½ cup (50 g) grated Parmigiano-Reggiano cheese

6 Preheat the oven to 400°F (200°C).

7 Spread 1½ cups (360 ml) of sauce over the bottom of a large lasagna pan. Arrange a layer of lasagna sheets, slightly overlapping one another, about 5 vertically and 1 horizontally, over the sauce. Cut any pieces that do not fit.

8 Spread about 1 cup (240 ml) of sauce over the pasta sheets. Top with one-third of the meatballs, ¼ cup (30 g) of the mozzarella, and 2 tablespoons of the Parmigiano-Reggiano. Repeat the layering 2 more times. Top the third layer of meatballs with a final layer of pasta sheets, 1½ cups (360 ml) of sauce, and the remaining Parmigiano-Reggiano.

9 Bake for 30 minutes. Sprinkle on the remaining mozzarella and bake until the cheese melts, about 10 minutes.

Nonna Dorotea Cristino's

ASTICE GRATINATO AL FORNO

LOBSTER OREGANATA

Prep time: 15 minutes
Cook time: 40 minutes
Yield: 2 to 4 servings

This easy yet impressive lobster dish is a great way to make your guests feel special on Christmas. Nonna Dorotea learned this recipe from her husband, Leonardo, who worked in an Italian-American restaurant while he was growing up in Brooklyn. "I remember the first time Lenny showed me how to split the lobster because I had never done it before, and I was a little scared. I worked on the bread-crumb topping for years, trying to get the right balance of oregano and garlic and cheese. I always like to make something special for Christmas, and this dish never disappoints."

2 live lobsters
6 tablespoons plain bread crumbs
2 tablespoons grated Pecorino Romano cheese
3 cloves garlic, minced
2 tablespoons minced fresh parsley
¼ cup (60 ml) extra-virgin olive oil
2 tablespoons dry white wine, such as Pinot Grigio
Lemon wedges, for serving

1. Place the lobsters, belly sides down, on a cutting board. Using a sharp knife, split the lobsters in half, straight down the middle, beginning with the point of the knife in the middle of the head and running it down the tail. Remove the eggs and the innards. Transfer the lobster halves, cut side up, to a rimmed baking sheet.
2. Preheat the oven to 400°F (200°C).
3. In a small bowl, stir together the bread crumbs, cheese, garlic, parsley, and olive oil. Spread the bread-crumb mixture over the lobsters and drizzle ½ tablespoon of wine over each half.
4. Add the ¾ cup (180 ml) of water to the baking sheet. Cover the sheet with aluminum foil and bake until the shells are red and the meat is firm, about 30 minutes. Uncover and bake for 10 minutes more.
5. Serve with lemon wedges for squeezing.

Nonna Laura Fosco's

GNOCCHI CON SUGO DI POMODORO

POTATO GNOCCHI WITH TOMATO SAUCE

Prep time: 40 minutes
Cook time: 1 hour
Yield: Makes 4 pounds (1.8 kg) gnocchi; 6 to 8 servings (see Nonna Laura Says)

Nonna Laura's ninety-year-old hands still work faster than someone a third of her age. "The gnocchi very eass', you see?" she says as she looks up at me, smiling while she rolls gnocchi horizontally across a wooden board so that they sort of resemble rigatoni. The light, pillowy dough isn't sticky to the touch when coated in flour, but it's moist on the inside, which will result in perfectly soft gnocchi. The general rule is the softer the dough, the softer the gnocchi, so try to resist adding too much flour if you can help it. She dresses them with a simple tomato sauce that really soaks into the gnocchi and hits that delicious Italian comfort-food spot.

SAUCE

3 tablespoons extra-virgin olive oil

3 cloves garlic, sliced

1 small onion, cut into ¼-inch (6 mm) dice

1 small carrot, cut into ¼-inch (6 mm) dice

3 ounces (85 g) tomato paste

24 ounces (680 g) passata or tomato puree

1 teaspoon salt

4 or 5 fresh basil leaves

GNOCCHI

3 pounds (1.4 kg) Idaho potatoes (about 4 potatoes), scrubbed and not peeled

1 large egg

1 tablespoon salted butter

1 teaspoon salt

3 cups (360 g) all-purpose or 00 flour, plus more for dusting

Grated Parmigiano-Reggiano cheese, for serving

1. **To make the sauce:** In a large skillet, heat the olive oil over medium heat. Add the garlic, onion, and carrot and cook, stirring occasionally, until the onion is translucent and the carrot is soft, 7 to 10 minutes. Add the tomato paste and cook, stirring occasionally, for 1 to 2 minutes. Stir in the passata, salt, and basil. Reduce the heat to low and simmer, uncovered, for 15 to 20 minutes.
2. **To make the gnocchi:** With a sharp knife, make a slit all the way around the skin of the potatoes. (Doing this will make the skin easier to remove after boiling.)
3. In a small stockpot, add the potatoes with enough cold water to cover them; bring to a boil over high heat. Cook the potatoes, uncovered, until fork-tender, 25 to 30 minutes. Drain and set aside to cool. When cool enough to handle, remove the skins.
4. Press the potatoes through a ricer into a large bowl. Add the egg, butter, and salt, and mix well.
5. Transfer the potato mixture to a floured surface. With your hands, incorporate the flour until fully absorbed and a supple dough forms. The dough should not stick to your hands.

6. Lightly flour a baking sheet. Take a chunk of dough and roll it into a rope about ½ inch (12 mm) thick. Line up 4 or 5 ropes of the same length and cut them into 1½ inch (4 cm) pieces. To give the gnocchi texture, they can be rolled over a gnocchi board, the back of a fork, or simply make an indentation with your finger. Place the gnocchi on the prepared baking sheet, making sure they don't touch. They can be cooked immediately or frozen.
7. **To freeze:** Place the baking sheet in the freezer until the gnocchi are frozen. Store in resealable plastic bags in the freezer for 2 to 3 months. Do not thaw before cooking.
8. **To cook the gnocchi:** Bring a large stockpot of generously salted water to a boil over high heat. Drop the gnocchi into the boiling water and cook just until they bob to the surface, 3 to 4 minutes. With a large slotted spoon, scoop out the gnocchi and add them to the tomato sauce. Cook, tossing, over medium-high heat, for 1 to 2 minutes. Serve in warm bowls with a generous sprinkle of grated Parmigiano-Reggiano.

Nonna Laura Says

This recipe makes about 4 pounds (1.8 kg) of gnocchi, which is quite a bit. My philosophy is that if I'm going to get the wooden board out and get my hands dirty to make something, I better make a lot. For this sauce recipe, I would only cook half the gnocchi, about 2 pounds (910 g), and freeze the rest. You never know when extra people will drop by for Sunday dinner!

Nonna Rosa Carmelo's

CARCIOFINI

BABY ARTICHOKES

Prep time: 10 minutes
Cook time: 40 minutes
Yield: 6 servings

Because my Nonno was an artichoke farmer in Italy, my family has always had a visceral connection to the vegetable. My Zia Rosa braises these babies in a white wine broth with a little garlic until they're tender and delicious, making them the perfect side dish or antipasto for a big family gathering.

- 2 pounds (910 g) baby artichokes (about 16)
- 2 lemons, halved, plus wedges for serving
- ½ cup (120 ml) extra-virgin olive oil
- 8 cloves garlic, sliced
- ½ cup (120 ml) dry white wine, such as Pinot Grigio
- 2 cups (480 ml) chicken broth
- 1 teaspoon salt
- 2 tablespoons minced fresh parsley

1. Fill a large bowl with cold water and set aside. Clean the artichokes by removing the outer leaves until you reach the yellow or light green parts; remove the stems and discard. Quarter the artichokes and add them to the bowl of cold water. Add the lemon halves to the bowl to prevent browning.
2. Heat the olive oil in a large skillet with a lid over medium heat. Add the garlic and cook, stirring occasionally, until golden, 1 to 2 minutes. Drain the artichokes and add them to the pan. Cook, stirring occasionally, for 5 minutes. Add the wine and cook, stirring occasionally, until the alcohol evaporates, about 2 minutes. Add the chicken broth and salt; bring to a boil over medium-high heat. Reduce the heat to low, cover the pan, and simmer until the artichokes are tender, 25 to 30 minutes.
3. Serve at room temperature with a sprinkle of parsley and a squeeze of fresh lemon juice.

Nonna Rosa Says

It is very important to use fresh artichokes for this recipe, as frozen ones will break down too much and become a little mooshad (mushy).

Nonna Vivian Cardia's

U TUCCU DI CARNE CON PANSOTTI ALLA LIGURE

GENOVESE MEAT SAUCE WITH SWISS CHARD-FILLED PASTA

Prep time: 1 hour
Cook time: 4 hours
Yield: 6 to 8 servings

When I asked Nonna Vivian about her favorite Ligurian Christmas recipes, *u tuccu* immediately came to her mind. The meat sauce is perfect served over fresh *pansotti*, which are filled with a mixture of Swiss chard and hard-boiled eggs. To save time, you can make the pansotti beforehand and freeze them.

SAUCE

1½ pounds (680 g) boneless bottom round beef (must be in 1 piece)

Salt and black pepper

1 ounce (28 g) dried porcini mushrooms

1 cup (240 ml) warm water

5 tablespoons extra-virgin olive oil

1 large onion, cut into ¼-inch (6 mm) dice

1 clove garlic

1 stalk celery, cut into ¼-inch (6 mm) dice

1 medium carrot, cut into ¼-inch (6 mm) dice

2 tablespoons minced fresh rosemary

¼ cup (34 g) pignoli (pine nuts), plus more for garnishing

½ cup (120 ml) dry red wine, such as Merlot

2 bay leaves

3 ounces (85 g) tomato paste

1 can (28 ounces/794 g) can crushed tomatoes

1 cup (240 ml) beef broth

1. **To make the sauce:** Season the beef well on all sides with salt and pepper.
2. In a small bowl, combine the mushrooms with the warm water. Let soak for 10 to 15 minutes to rehydrate. With a slotted spoon, transfer the mushrooms to a cutting board; finely chop. Pour the soaking water through a fine-mesh strainer lined with paper towels into a small bowl.
3. In a Dutch oven or large heavy-bottomed pot over medium-high heat, combine the olive oil, onion, garlic, celery, carrot, and rosemary. Cook, stirring occasionally, for 3 to 5 minutes. Add the meat and brown very well on all sides, 8 to 10 minutes. (This is the most important step.) Add the chopped mushrooms and pignoli and cook, stirring occasionally, for 2 to 3 minutes. Add the wine and the bay leaves and cook, stirring occasionally, until the alcohol evaporates, 2 to 3 minutes. Stir in the tomato paste and cook for 1 minute. Stir in the crushed tomatoes, broth, and the reserved mushroom soaking water. Bring to a boil over medium-high heat, then reduce the heat to the lowest level possible. Cover the pan and simmer until the meat is easily shredded with a fork, about 3 hours and 30 minutes. Check on the sauce often, stirring with a wooden spoon and turning the meat over to prevent it from sticking.
4. **Meanwhile, make the pasta filling:** Bring a large stockpot of lightly salted water to a boil over high heat. Drop in the Swiss chard and boil until tender, 15 to 20 minutes. Drain and run under cold water. Squeeze out the excess water and transfer it to a food processor fitted with the blade attachment. Add the Pecorino Romano, pignoli, hard-cooked eggs, and dried marjoram and process until smooth, about 10 seconds. Transfer to a medium bowl.

PASTA FILLING

Salt

1 bunch Swiss chard, washed and ends trimmed

1 cup (100 g) grated Pecorino Romano cheese, plus more for serving

¼ cup (34 g) pignoli (pine nuts)

2 large hard-cooked eggs, peeled

1 teaspoon dried marjoram

PASTA DOUGH

2½ cups (300 g) all-purpose or 00 flour

3 large eggs, at room temperature, well beaten

1 large egg yolk, at room temperature, well beaten

¼ teaspoon salt, plus more to taste

5 **To make the pasta dough:** In the bowl of a stand mixer fitted with the dough hook attachment, mix the flour, eggs, egg yolk, and salt at low speed until incorporated and a dough forms, 5 to 6 minutes.

6 Turn out the dough onto a clean work surface and begin kneading with your hands, picking up any particles of dough as you go. If the dough feels dry, add 1 tablespoon of tepid water at a time until it comes together. Continue kneading until the dough is smooth and supple and has the consistency of play dough, 8 to 10 minutes. Wrap the dough ball in plastic wrap and let rest at room temperature for 30 minutes.

7 Divide the dough into 4 equal pieces. Working one piece at a time, using a rolling pin, roll them into a rectangle as thin as possible, you can almost see through them, about ⅛ or 1⁄16 inch (3 or 1 mm) thick. Cover any dough sheets not being used with a clean, damp kitchen towel.

8 Lightly flour a baking sheet. Begin working on the longer horizontal edge of one rectangle. Dot 1 teaspoon of filling along one side of the dough about 1½ inches (4 cm) apart, leaving at least a ½-inch (12 mm) border on all sides. Dip your finger in water and dampen the area around the filling. Fold the dough over to cover the filling. Press down on the edges of the dough and press together the areas around the filling with your fingers to create separate pockets of filling. With a ravioli cutter, cut out 2-inch (5 cm) squares and transfer to the prepared baking sheet, arranging them in a single layer. They can be cooked immediately or frozen.

9 **To freeze:** Place the baking sheet in the freezer until the squares are frozen. Store in resealable plastic bags in the freezer for 2 to 3 months. Do not thaw before cooking.

10 **To cook the pasta:** Bring the sauce to a simmer over medium heat. Bring a large stockpot of generously salted water to a boil over high heat. Drop the pasta into the boiling water. Cook until al dente, about 5 minutes. Scoop the pasta out and add it to the sauce. Cook, tossing, for 1 to 2 minutes.

11 Serve in warm bowls with an extra sprinkle of Pecorino Romano and garnish with a few pignoli. Break up the meat and either serve atop the pasta or, traditionally, as an entrée.

Nonna Vivian Says

Sprinkle a few extra pignoli nuts around the dishes when serving for an effortlessly elegant presentation.

Nonna Rosetta Rauseo's

MOSTACCIOLI

ALMOND SPICE COOKIES WITH CHOCOLATE

Prep time: 45 minutes
Cook time: 12 minutes
Yield: About 40 cookies

Mostaccioli are a popular Christmas cookie in southern Italy, especially among those who hail from the Campania region. Nonna Rosetta's are the perfect blend of spicy and chocolatey goodness, with a pop of crunch from the toasted almonds. She garnishes them with a swipe of melted semisweet chocolate that dries to a shiny finish and adds some sparkle to every Christmas cookie tray!

COOKIES

½ cup (73 g) whole almonds

2 cups plus 1 tablespoon (248 g) all-purpose or 00 flour, plus more for dusting

2½ tablespoons unsweetened cocoa powder

1½ teaspoons baking powder

¾ teaspoon ground cinnamon

½ teaspoon ground cloves

2 large eggs

½ cup (170 g) honey

½ cup (100 g) sugar

Zest of 1 orange

Zest of 1 lemon

Nonstick cooking spray, for greasing

GLAZE

8 ounces (225 g) good-quality semisweet chocolate

1. **To make the cookies:** Preheat the oven to 400°F (200°C). Spread the almonds on a baking sheet and toast until fragrant, 7 to 8 minutes. Coarsely chop the toasted almonds and set aside.
2. In a large bowl, whisk together the flour, cocoa, baking powder, cinnamon, and cloves. Add the chopped almonds and whisk to combine.
3. In another large bowl, whisk together the eggs, honey, sugar, orange zest, and lemon zest. Add this mixture to the dry ingredients and mix with a wooden spoon or spatula until a dough forms. Cover the bowl with plastic wrap and let rest at room temperature for 30 minutes.
4. Preheat the oven to 350°F (180°C). Line a baking sheet with parchment paper or aluminum foil and lightly grease it with nonstick cooking spray.
5. Lightly flour a clean work surface and turn the dough out onto it. Flour a rolling pin and roll out the dough ¼ inch (6 mm) thick. If the dough is sticky, keep dusting the surface and the dough with flour.
6. Using a 2½ by 3-inch (6 by 7.5 cm) rhomboid-shaped cookie cutter, cut out the cookies. Reroll any scraps and continue cutting cookies until all the dough is used. Place the cookies on the prepared baking sheet.
7. Bake until the bottoms of the cookies color, 10 to 12 minutes. Let cool completely before dipping in the glaze.
8. **To make the glaze:** Melt the chocolate in a double boiler or a microwave. Dip the tops of each cookie into the melted chocolate and let cool on a wire rack.

Nonna Michelina Gagliardo's

CUCCIDDATI

SICILIAN FIG COOKIES

Prep time: 1 hour
Cook time: 24 minutes
Yield: About 48 cookies

No self-respecting Sicilian can let a Christmas go by without making these delightful fig-filled cookies. All throughout Sicily, you will find slight variations on this cookie's filling and shape. Every family seems to have their own precious recipe that they safeguard against outsiders. Luckily, Zia Michelina was sweet enough to give up the goods: "*Ti do questa ricetta che è beautiful troppo assai, bedda Mia!* (I'll give you this recipe that is too beautiful, my love!)" At her house, making *cucciddati* is a family event, where all her daughters and granddaughters pitch in. Zia Michelina says you can make the filling up to two weeks in advance and chill it in the refrigerator: "*Cosi pigghia u sappuri.* (So it absorbs the flavor.)" The cookies are wonderful eaten plain—as is more common in Italy—as well as coated with a sweet glaze and sprinkled with rainbow nonpareils.

FILLING

14 ounces (400 g) dried figs, stemmed
1¼ cups (180 g) raisins
½ cup (90 g) mini semisweet chocolate chips
1 tablespoon Grand Marnier, Cointreau, or another orange-flavored liqueur
1 tablespoon cold espresso coffee
1 teaspoon ground cinnamon
Zest of 1 orange

DOUGH

2½ cups (300 g) all-purpose or 00 flour
1¼ cups (205 g) semolina flour
2 teaspoons baking powder
1 cup (200 g) granulated sugar
1 cup (225 g) shortening
2 large eggs, at room temperature
¼ cup (60 ml) whole milk

1. **To make the filling:** In a large saucepan, combine the figs with enough cold water to cover them completely. Bring to a boil over medium-high heat and cook until the figs are soft, about 10 minutes. Drain and let cool to room temperature.
2. **Meanwhile make the dough:** In a large bowl, whisk together the all-purpose flour, semolina, and baking powder.
3. In the bowl of a stand mixer fitted with the paddle attachment, beat the granulated sugar and shortening at medium speed until fluffy, about 5 minutes. Add the eggs, one at a time, and mix at medium speed until fully incorporated before adding the next. Add the milk and mix at medium speed to combine. With the mixer at low speed, add the dry ingredients; mix at low speed until a dough forms and pulls away from the sides of the bowl. Divide the dough into 4 equal pieces and flatten them into disks. Wrap each disk in plastic wrap and refrigerate until firm, about 1 hour.
4. Place the cooled figs in a food processor fitted with the blade attachment along with the raisins, chocolate chips, Grand Marnier, coffee, cinnamon, and orange zest. Process until smooth, about 20 seconds.

CONTINUED ON PAGE 158

CONTINUED FROM PAGE 156

GLAZE

2 cups (240 g) confectioners' sugar

½ teaspoon vanilla extract

2 tablespoons (30 ml) whole milk

Rainbow nonpareils, for decorating

5 **To assemble:** Preheat the oven to 375°F (190°C). Line two baking sheets with parchment paper.

6 Unwrap one disk of chilled dough (keep the others refrigerated) and roll it into a rectangle about 3½ inches (9 cm) by 14 inches (36 cm) and ⅛inch (3 mm) thick. Place a 1-inch-wide (2.5 cm) log of filling in the center of the dough, leaving about a 1-inch (2.5 cm) border at the top and bottom. Take one side of the dough and roll it over, enclosing the filling to make a log. (Don't worry if there are a few cracks in the cookies; they will be covered when you ice them.) Pinch the ends together to seal.

7 Using a sharp floured knife, cut out cookies 2 inches (5 cm) long, making diagonal cuts so each cookie is shaped like a diamond. Place them, seam side down, on the prepared baking sheets, about 1 inch (2.5 cm) apart. Continue with the remaining dough and filling.

8 Bake until the bottoms are nicely browned, 12 to 14 minutes. Let cool completely before glazing.

9 **To make the glaze:** In a small bowl, whisk together the confectioners' sugar, vanilla, and milk. Drizzle the glaze over the cooled cookies and sprinkle with rainbow nonpareils.

Nonna Romana Sciddurlo's

TORRONE DI MANDORLE

PUGLIESE CANDIED ALMONDS

Prep time: 20 minutes
Cook time: 30 minutes
Yield: About 36 squares

Every holiday season, Nonna Romana and my Zia Rosa turn my Nonna's basement-apartment kitchen into a veritable commercial bakery, producing enough holiday sweets that seem to last until New Year's Eve. One of their most popular confections is a classic Pugliese *torrone di mandorle*, which differs greatly from a classic nougat found in many regions of Italy. This torrone is actually more of an almond brittle—super crunchy, not too sweet, and a gorgeous deep-amber color. The secret ingredient is a little bit of white vinegar, which my great-grandmother Regina began adding because she swore it made the torrone better. I'm going to be totally real with you: To this day we have no idea what exactly the vinegar does, but no one wants to mess with tradition, and if it's not broken . . . don't fix it.

2 cups (290 g) raw almonds
1 cup (200 g) sugar
2 tablespoons white vinegar
Zest of 1 lemon
2 cups (290 g) raw almonds
2 tablespoons white vinegar
Zest of 1 lemon

1. Line a flat surface with a large sheet of aluminum foil.
2. In a small stockpot, add the almonds, sugar, vinegar, lemon zest, and ¼ cup (60 ml) of water and cook, stirring with a wooden spoon, over medium heat. The sugar will melt, but you must keep stirring continuously until the sugar crystalizes again, 10 to 15 minutes. Continue to stir until the sugar melts once again and turns a dark amber color, 10 to 15 minutes.
3. Remove from the heat and pour the contents onto the foil. With a spatula, quickly flatten the hot almonds to form a sheet about ¾ inch (2 cm) thick. Let cool for about 5 minutes.
4. With a large knife, cut the entire sheet into 2-inch (5 cm) squares. Remove the aluminum foil from all the pieces and cool completely before serving.

Nonna Romana Scidduro's

CARTELLATE

PUGLIESE CHRISTMAS FRITTERS

Prep time: 1 hour

Cook time: 6 hours 30 minutes

Yield: About 48 cartellate

"*Se non facciamo le cartellate, non mi sembra che è Natale* (If we don't make *cartellate*, it doesn't feel like Christmas)," my Nonna Romana declares every year the day after Thanksgiving. These traditional fritters are the most popular Christmas dessert from the region of Puglia. Cartellate with vin cotto are best when made and dipped a day or so before serving, as the flavor of the vin cotto intensifies. Undipped, the cartellate can be kept in an airtight container for a few weeks.

CARTELLATE

3 cups (360 g) all-purpose or 00 flour

1 cup (240 ml) white wine, such as Pinot Grigio or Chablis

¼ cup (60 ml) olive oil

Oil, for frying

DIPPING SAUCE

1 cup (240 ml) Vin Cotto (page 9)

Ground cinnamon, for sprinkling

OR

1½ cups (510 g) honey

Rainbow sprinkles, for decorating

1. **To make the cartellate:** Place the flour on a clean work surface and make a well in the center Add the wine and oil to the well and begin incorporating the flour into the liquid until fully absorbed. Knead with your hands until a supple dough forms, 8 to 10 minutes.
2. Using a pasta roller, begin passing golf ball-size chunks of dough through it at a #3 setting. Fold the dough over and keep passing it through until the sheets no longer have holes. Once you achieve smooth sheets of dough, transfer them to a clean work surface. Using a ravioli cutter, cut strips of dough about 10 to 12 inches (25 to 30 cm) long and 1½ inches (4 cm) wide. Cover any unused dough with a clean, damp kitchen towel. (Once the sheets dry too much, they will be difficult to pinch together.)
3. Flip the strips of dough to the wetter side and fold the end up at one side, about 1 inch (2.5 cm), pinching it together. Pinch the dough together the same way, every inch (2.5 cm) or so, creating little pockets. Roll the strip into a pinwheel and pinch the pockets together as you roll. This creates the pockets that will hold the vin cotto or honey. Place the rolled cartellate on a clean kitchen towel.
4. Line a plate with paper towels. In a small stockpot, heat 2 inches (5 cm) of oil over high heat. Working in batches, fry the cartellate until golden brown, about 2 minutes per batch. Transfer to the prepared plate.
5. **To dip:** In a large saucepan, bring the vin cotto or the honey to a simmer over medium heat. Using a fork, dip the cartellate until completely coated. Transfer to a serving dish and sprinkle the vin cotto-dipped cartellate with a dash of cinnamon; sprinkle the honey-dipped cartellate with sprinkles as desired.

Nonna Rosa Virone's

TURDILLI

CALABRESE HONEY BALLS

Prep time: 45 minutes
Cook time: 30 minutes
Yield: About 200 honey balls

Turdilli are small fritters of dough made with wine, and are typical of Calabria. They are fried and then dipped in warm honey, and decorated with colorful sprinkles. You can make these with white or red wine, but Nonna Rosa prefers red because it gives the dough a purple tint.

1 cup (240 ml) sweet red wine
½ cup (120 ml) vegetable oil
½ teaspoon lemon extract
¼ teaspoon sugar
Pinch salt
1 large egg
3 cups (360 g) all-purpose or 00 flour, plus more for dusting
¼ teaspoon baking powder
Oil, for frying
3 cups (720 ml) honey, plus more as needed
Rainbow nonpareils, for decorating

1. In a small saucepan, bring the wine, vegetable oil, lemon extract, sugar, and salt to a boil over high heat. Remove from the heat and let cool for 15 minutes.
2. In the bowl of a stand mixer fitted with the paddle attachment, mix the cooled wine mixture and the egg at medium speed until combined. With the mixer at low speed, add the flour and baking powder, a little at a time. Mix until a soft, tacky dough forms.
3. Lightly flour a clean work surface and turn the dough out onto it. Knead the dough by hand until smooth and supple, about 5 minutes. Cover the dough with a clean kitchen towel and let rest for 10 minutes.
4. Divide the dough into 8 pieces. Roll each piece into a ½-inch-thick (13 mm) rope. Cut the rope into pieces about 1½ inches (4 cm) long. Roll each piece on the back of a fork or a gnocchi board.
5. Line a plate with paper towels. In a large saucepan, heat about 2½ inches (6.5 cm) of oil over high heat. Working in batches, fry the balls until golden brown, 2 to 3 minutes per batch. With a slotted spoon, transfer to the prepared plate.
6. In a small saucepan over low heat, warm the honey until liquid. Toss the balls, a handful at a time, in the honey to coat. With a slotted spoon, transfer to a serving dish. Sprinkle with the nonpareils.

Nonna Annita Fallone Apruzzese's

BISCOTTI AL VINO

WINE COOKIES

Prep time: 10 minutes
Cook time: 15 minutes
Yield: About 35 cookies

"When you bake the wine cookies, the whole house smells beautiful!" Nonna Annita says, as I help her dip a little bagel-shaped cookie into granulated sugar, while the intoxicating aroma of sweet wine and fennel seeds waft past me from the baking sheet in the oven. These simple, slightly sweet wine cookies are typical of Nonna Annita's hometown of Ciociaria, and their mild flavor makes them perfect for dipping in a glass of wine or in your morning coffee. You can use red or white wine for this recipe, but Nonna Annita prefers to use white wine (which she makes herself) for a lighter flavor.

- 2 cups (240 g) all-purpose or 00 flour
- 2 teaspoons baking powder
- ½ cup (120 ml) white wine, any kind you like
- 6 tablespoons extra-virgin olive oil, plus more for working the dough
- ½ cup (100 g) sugar, plus more for dipping the cookies
- 1 tablespoon fennel seeds

1. Preheat the oven to 400°F (200°C). Line 2 baking sheets with parchment paper.
2. In a medium bowl, whisk together the flour and baking powder.
3. In the bowl of a stand mixer fitted with the paddle attachment, mix the wine, olive oil, and sugar at medium-high speed until the sugar dissolves. Add the fennel seeds and mix until combined. Add half of the dry ingredients to the bowl and mix at low speed until absorbed. Add the remaining dry ingredients and mix at low speed, just until absorbed.
4. Pour some sugar into a shallow dish.
5. Oil your hands and roll a chunk of dough into a rope about 4 inches (10 cm) long and ½ inch (12 mm) thick. Bring the ends together to form a ring. Roll one side of the ring in the sugar and place it, sugared side up, on the prepared baking sheets. Continue with the remaining dough, placing the cookies 2 inches (5 cm) apart.
6. Bake until the cookies are golden, about 15 minutes.

Nonna Annita Fallone Apruzzese's

BISCOTTI CON FORMAGGIO CREMOSO

CREAM CHEESE KNOT COOKIES

Prep time: 15 minutes
Cook time: 45 minutes
Yield: About 60 cookies

While these delectable little knot cookies aren't an example of traditional Italian baking, they are highly addictive! All of Nonna Annita's grandchildren look forward to the holiday season, when they help her make hundreds of cookies for her church group in Jersey City. The cookies themselves are lightly sweetened and flavored with a tiny bit of anise liqueur (she's partial to Marie Brizard), which she also adds to the glaze for a little kick. It is the holiday season, after all!

COOKIES

3 cups (360 g) all-purpose or 00 flour

1 tablespoon baking powder

4 ounces (113 g) cream cheese, at room temperature

½ cup (1 stick/120 g) unsalted butter, at room temperature

½ cup (100 g) granulated sugar

2 large eggs

2 tablespoons anisette liqueur or anise extract

1 packet (½ ounce/15 g) Italian vanilla powder or 1 teaspoon vanilla extract

GLAZE

3 cups (360 g) confectioners' sugar

3 tablespoons anisette liqueur or anise extract

¼ cup (60 ml) whole milk

Nonpareils, for decorating

1. **To make the cookies:** Preheat the oven to 350°F (180°C). Line two 13 by 18-inch (33 by 46 cm) baking sheets with parchment paper.
2. In a large bowl, whisk together the flour and baking powder.
3. In the bowl of a stand mixer fitted with the paddle attachment, mix the cream cheese, butter, and granulated sugar at medium speed until fluffy, about 5 minutes. Add the eggs, one at a time, mixing until each one is fully incorporated. Add the anisette and vanilla; mix to combine. With the mixer at low speed, add the flour-baking powder mixture, and mix until fully absorbed and a soft dough forms.
4. On a clean work surface, roll a chunk of dough into a rope about ½ inch (12 mm) thick. Cut the rope into 4- to 5-inch-long (10 to 12.5 cm) pieces. Shape into little knots and place on the prepared baking sheet about 2 inches (5 cm) apart.
5. Bake until the cookies just begin to color, 10 to 15 minutes. Let cool completely before glazing.
6. **To make the glaze:** In a small bowl, whisk together the confectioners' sugar, anisette, and milk until smooth. Drizzle the glaze over the cooled cookies and decorate with the nonpareils.

Nonna Rosa Virone's

PITTA 'MPIGLIATA

CALABRESE FRUIT AND NUT PASTRY

Prep time: 45 minutes

Cook time: 45 minutes

Yield: One 9-inch (23 cm) pitta

In Nonna Rosa's family, they call this Christmas confection *rosette*, or "little roses," because strips of shortbread are spread with a layer of prunes, raisins, and walnuts, and rolled up into rosettes. Nonna Rosa loves this recipe because, when it comes to the fruits and nuts used, "you can use whateva you like-a!"

DOUGH

1 cup (240 ml) dry white wine

1/4 cup (60 ml) olive oil

1/4 cup (50 g) sugar

1 packet (1/2 ounce/15 g) Italian vanilla powder or 1 teaspoon vanilla extract

3 large eggs, divided

3 3/4 cups (450 g) all-purpose or 00 flour, plus more for dusting

2 teaspoons baking powder

Nonstick cooking spray, for greasing

FILLING

1 cup (100 g) walnuts

1/2 cup (87.5 g) pitted prunes

1/2 cup (75 g) raisins

Zest of 1 orange

1 tablespoon honey

1 tablespoon vermouth

1/2 teaspoon ground cinnamon

1/4 teaspoon ground cloves

BRUSHING

1/4 cup (80 g) apricot preserves

Rainbow nonpareils, for decorating

1. **To make the dough:** In the bowl of a stand mixer fitted with the paddle attachment, mix the wine, olive oil, sugar, and vanilla at medium speed until combined. Add 2 of the eggs and mix at medium speed until incorporated. Change the attachment to the dough hook. Add the flour and baking powder, and mix again at medium speed until a smooth dough comes together, 3 to 5 minutes.
2. Lightly flour a work surface and turn the dough out onto it. Knead by hand for 2 to 3 minutes. Cover the dough with a clean kitchen towel and let rest while you make the filling.
3. **To make the filling:** In a food processor fitted with the blade attachment, process the walnuts, prunes, raisins, orange zest, honey, vermouth, cinnamon, and cloves until no large chunks remain, 20 to 30 seconds. Transfer to a medium bowl.
4. Preheat the oven to 350°F (180°C). Grease a 9-inch (23 cm) pie plate with cooking spray.
5. With a rolling pin, roll one-third of the dough into a 10-inch (25 cm) circle about 1/8 inch (3 mm) thick; transfer it to the pie plate. Trim any excess to the height of the pie plate.
6. Roll the remaining dough 1/3 inch (3 mm) thick. Using a ravioli cutter, cut 12 to 13 strips, about 10 to 12 inches (25 to 30 cm) long and 2 inches (5 cm) wide. Spread the filling along each strip and roll into a rosette. Place the first rosette in the middle of the crust. Place each additional rosette around the first one. Fold in the surrounding dough.
7. Beat the remaining egg and brush the entire pastry with it. Bake until golden brown, 40 to 45 minutes.
8. **For brushing:** In a small saucepan over medium heat, combine the apricot preserves and 2 tablespoons of water. Heat until liquid. Brush the pitta with the preserves and decorate with the nonpareils.

Nonna Antoinette Capodicci's

STRUFFOLI CONES

Prep time: 1 hour
Cook time: 15 minutes
Yield: 8 to 10 cones

Struffoli are Neapolitan honey balls that are synonymous with celebrating Christmas, Italian-style. But let's be real: They can be a bit messy to eat. One year, the ever-clever Nonna Antoinette had the brilliant idea of serving them in ice-cream cones to cut down on the sticky factor and give them a festive presentation, perfect for any holiday dessert bar. The kids are sure to love them too!

STRUFFOLI

3 cups (360 g) all-purpose or 00 flour, plus more for dusting

½ teaspoon baking powder

Pinch salt

2 tablespoons unsalted butter, softened

2 tablespoons sugar

4 large eggs, at room temperature

1 teaspoon vanilla extract

1 tablespoon white wine

Zest of ½ lemon

Zest of ½ orange

Olive oil, for frying (or use any frying oil you like)

Small ice cream cones

Rainbow Jimmies or nonpareils, to decorate

HONEY SYRUP

1½ cups (510 g) honey

½ cup (100 g) sugar

1. **To make the struffoli:** In a medium bowl, whisk together the flour, baking powder, and salt.
2. In the bowl of a stand mixer fitted with the paddle attachment, beat the butter and sugar at medium speed until fluffy, about 5 minutes. With the mixer at low speed, add the eggs, one at a time, mixing until fully incorporated before adding the next, then add the vanilla, wine, lemon zest, and orange zest. Add the dry ingredients and mix until a slightly firm dough comes together, 3 to 4 minutes.
3. Flour a clean work surface and a baking sheet. Take a small chunk of dough, and with your hands, roll it into a long rope about ½ inch (12 mm) thick. With a knife, cut the rope into ¼-inch (6 mm) pieces. Roll the pieces into balls and place them on the prepared baking sheet. Repeat with the remaining dough.
4. Line a plate with paper towels. In a large saucepan, heat about 1½ inches (4 cm) of olive oil over medium-high heat until it reaches about 350°F (180°C). Working in small batches, fry the dough balls until light golden brown, 2 to 3 minutes per batch. Transfer to the prepared plate.
5. **To make the honey syrup:** In another large saucepan, bring the honey, sugar, and 2 tablespoons of water to a boil over medium heat.
6. Working in small batches, drop in the struffoli. With a slotted spoon, stir them in the honey until they are completely coated, then transfer to a serving plate. Allow the struffoli to become a little bit tacky before, using 2 spoons, transferring them to the cones and shaping them into small mounds. Decorate with the sprinkles.

Nonna Romana Sciddurlo's

PANETTONE

ITALIAN CHRISTMAS BREAD

Prep time: 30 hours
Cook time: 45 minutes
Yield: One 6-inch (15 cm) panettone

There are a few things Italians could possibly live without at Christmastime, but *panettone* is not one of them. This lightly sweetened fruit and nut bread is, without a doubt, the official symbol of an Italian Christmas. Nonna Romana's panettone isn't too sweet, making it perfect for a little after-dinner snack or with morning coffee after it dries out a bit. Making your own panettone is a bit of a labor of love and will take up some time, but it will leave you with a sense of accomplishment and the house smelling like Christmas.

BIGA

2 tablespoons (24 g) active dry yeast

¼ cup plus 3 tablespoons (105 ml) lukewarm water

¾ cup (98 g) Manitoba flour

FIRST MIX

3 large egg yolks

1 large egg

1½ cups (195 g) Manitoba flour, plus more for dusting

¼ cup (50 g) sugar

⅓ cup (80 ml) whole milk

1 tablespoon (20 g) molasses

3½ tablespoons (53 g) unsalted butter, cut into pieces, at room temperature

SECOND MIX

½ cup (75 g) golden raisins

½ cup (75 g) raisins

3 tablespoons (45 ml) white rum

Dough, from the first rising

Remaining eggs from the first mix

⅓ cup plus 1 tablespoon (80 g) sugar

1. **To make the biga:** In a small bowl, dissolve the yeast in the lukewarm water, stirring, for 5 minutes. Add the flour and mix with your hands until a very sticky dough ball forms. Transfer the dough to a clean bowl and cover with plastic wrap. Refrigerate for 5 hours.
2. Remove the bowl from the refrigerator and let stand at room temperature for 2 hours.
3. **To make the first mix:** Measure 3 ounces (85 g) of biga. Refrigerate the remaining biga to use as a starter for other baking.
4. In a small bowl, whisk together the egg yolks and egg. Measure the volume of the eggs and reserve half in the refrigerator for the second mix.
5. In the bowl of a stand mixer fitted with the dough hook attachment, mix the biga, half the whisked eggs, the flour, sugar, milk, and molasses at medium speed for 5 minutes. Add the butter, 1 tablespoon (15 g) at a time, mixing at medium speed after each addition until it is fully absorbed before adding the next.
6. Lightly flour a work surface and turn the dough out onto it. Flour your hands and knead the dough by hand for 5 minutes. If the dough feels sticky, continue to flour the work surface. Transfer to a large bowl and cover it with plastic wrap. Let rest in a warm place for 12 hours.
7. **To make the second mix:** In a small bowl, combine the raisins, water, and rum and let soak for 2 hours. Drain and discard the soaking liquid. Pat the raisins dry with paper towels.

1 packet (½ ounce/15 g) Italian vanilla powder or 1 teaspoon vanilla extract

Zest of 1 orange

Zest of 1 lemon

Zest of 1 tangerine

1 cup plus 2½ tablespoons (150 g) Manitoba flour

¼ cup (½ stick/60 g) unsalted butter

8 Punch down the dough and transfer it to the bowl of a stand mixer fitted with the dough hook attachment. Add the reserved half of the whisked eggs, the sugar, vanilla, orange zest, lemon zest, tangerine zest, and flour; mix at medium speed for 5 minutes. Add the butter, 1 tablespoon (15 g) at a time, mixing at medium speed after each addition until it is fully absorbed before adding the next. When the butter is fully absorbed, add the soaked raisins and mix at medium speed for 5 minutes.

9 Lightly flour a wooden board and transfer the dough to it. Knead by hand until the dough is elastic, 7 to 10 minutes. Shape the dough into a ball and place it, smooth side down, in a paper panettone mold. Cover the mold with plastic wrap and let rest in a warm place until the dough doubles in size and rises about 2 inches (5 cm) below the top of the mold, 6 to 7 hours.

10 When the dough has just about doubled, remove the plastic wrap and let sit, uncovered, for 30 minutes.

11 Preheat the oven to 350°F (180°C). Score a cross across the top of the dough. Place the panettone mold onto a baking sheet and bake until golden brown and springy in the middle, about 45 minutes.

Nonna Laura Fosco's

PIZZELLE AL LIMONE

ITALIAN LEMON WAFFLE COOKIES

Prep time: 10 minutes

Cook time: 1 hour

Yield: About 50 cookies

In Italian-American culture, pizzelle have become synonymous with Christmastime. Nonna Laura hails from the region of Abruzzo, where *pizzelle* originated, and there, they are made year-round using a simple batter that can have different flavorings, the most popular being anise. Nonna Laura flavors hers with her homemade Sweet Lemon Zest (page 8) and makes them two at a time using her trusty electric iron in her Queens basement. They're exquisite, with a simple dusting of powdered sugar, and no matter how many she makes, they don't last long.

- 6 large eggs
- ¾ cup plus 1 tablespoon (163 g) sugar
- ½ cup (120 ml) vegetable oil, plus more for greasing
- 1 teaspoon vanilla extract
- Zest of 1 lemon
- Juice of 1 lemon or 1 tablespoon Nonna Laura's Sweet Lemon Zest (page 8)
- 1¾ cups plus 1 tablespoon (310 g) all-purpose or 00 flour
- 2 teaspoons baking powder

1. In a large bowl, using a handheld electric mixer, beat the eggs, sugar, oil, vanilla, lemon zest, and lemon juice at high speed until smooth. Add the flour and baking powder and mix at high speed for 30 seconds. Give the batter a good stir with a spoon or a spatula.
2. Preheat a pizzelle iron until very hot. Moisten a paper towel with vegetable oil and carefully grease the hot iron.
3. Add 1 tablespoon of batter to each cavity and close the iron. Cook until the cookies are golden, 1 to 2 minutes. Using a fork, carefully lift the cookies off the iron and transfer to a baking sheet in a single layer. Let cool completely.

Nonna Laura Says

The pizzelle are very soft when you first make them, but as they cool, they have a nice, crispy texture, like waffles. It's best if you leave them to cool in a single layer to prevent them from getting soggy.

Nonna Vivian Cardia's

Canestrelli di Torriglia

LIGURIAN BUTTER COOKIES

Prep time: 20 minutes
Cook time: 18 minutes
Yield: About 36 cookies

When it comes to Christmas cookies, Nonna Vivian keeps it simple and chic with these classic Ligurian butter cookies. *Canestrelli* is an easy shortbread recipe that has a hint of lemon and white rum. The cookies are then cut into a lovely daisy shape with a cookie cutter and dusted with a light coating of powdered sugar.

1 cup (2 sticks/240 g) unsalted butter, at room temperature, plus more for greasing

6 tablespoons granulated sugar

2 large egg yolks, at room temperature

Zest of ½ lemon or 2 teaspoons Nonna Laura's Sweet Lemon Zest (page 8)

1 packet (½ ounce/15 g) Italian vanilla powder or 1 teaspoon vanilla extract

1 tablespoon white rum

1½ cups (180 g) all-purpose or 00 flour

¾ cup (96 g) cornstarch

Confectioners' sugar, for dusting

1. In the bowl of a stand mixer fitted with the paddle attachment, beat the butter and granulated sugar at high speed until fluffy, about 5 minutes. Add the egg yolks, one at a time, mixing at medium speed until fully incorporated before adding the next. Add the lemon zest, vanilla, and rum; mix at medium speed to combine. With the mixer running at low speed, add the flour and cornstarch; mix until a soft dough forms.
2. Spread the dough onto a piece of plastic wrap and flatten into a disk. Refrigerate until firm, about 1 hour.
3. Preheat the oven to 340°F (171°C). Grease a baking sheet with butter.
4. Place the dough between two pieces of parchment paper and roll it ¼ inch (6 mm) thick, using rolling guides to help, if you have them. Chill any dough not being used.
5. Using a 2½-inch (6 cm) daisy-shaped cookie cutter, cut out the cookies and place them 1 inch (2.5 cm) apart on the prepared baking sheet. Optionally, cut out the centers with a small round cookie cutter. Place the baking sheet in the freezer for 5 minutes before baking.
6. Bake until the cookies have just slightly colored on the bottom and the tops are still quite pale, 15 to 18 minutes. Let cool completely. Dust with confectioners' sugar.

Nonna Nina Labruna's

BISCOTTI AL CIOCCOLATO E ARANCIA CON NOCCIOLE

CHOCOLATE-ORANGE-HAZELNUT BISCOTTI

Prep time: 20 minutes
Cook time: 1 hour 10 minutes
Yield: About 40 biscotti

- 2 cups (240 g) all-purpose or 00 flour
- ⅓ cup plus 2 tablespoons (39 g) unsweetened cocoa powder
- 1½ tablespoons ground espresso powder
- 1 teaspoon baking soda
- ½ teaspoon salt
- ¼ cup (½ stick/60 g) unsalted butter, at room temperature
- 1 cup (225 g) packed brown sugar
- 1 packet (½ ounce/15 g) Italian vanilla powder or 1 teaspoon vanilla extract
- 3 large eggs
- Zest of 2 oranges
- 1½ teaspoons orange extract
- 3 ounces (85 g) good-quality semisweet chocolate, finely chopped
- 1 cup (115 g) chopped hazelnuts

An excellent chocolate biscotti recipe is a necessity for holiday baking. Nonna Nina's have some hazelnuts and a hint of orange and are delectable when dipped in strong espresso or some Vin Santo for dessert.

1. Preheat the oven to 300°F (150°C). Line a baking sheet with parchment paper.
2. In a medium bowl, whisk together the flour, cocoa powder, espresso powder, baking soda, and salt.
3. In the bowl of a stand mixer fitted with the paddle attachment, beat the butter, brown sugar, and vanilla at medium-high speed until fluffy, about 5 minutes. Add the eggs, one at a time, mixing at medium speed until fully incorporated before adding the next. Add the orange zest and extract; mix at medium speed to combine. Add half of the dry ingredients and mix at low speed until absorbed. Add the chocolate, hazelnuts, and the remaining dry ingredients; mix at low speed until a dough forms.
4. Divide the dough into 2 equal pieces and place them on the prepared baking sheet. Shape each piece into a log about 14 inches (36 cm) long and 2½ inches (6 cm) wide. Bake until the logs feel firm to the touch, about 30 minutes. Let cool for 15 minutes.
5. Using a serrated knife, cut the logs crosswise into 1-inch-thick (2.5 cm) slices. Place the slices, cut side down, onto 2 baking sheets. Bake for 15 to 20 minutes. Flip the biscotti and bake for 15 to 20 minutes more. The longer you bake the biscotti, the crispier they will be.

Nonna Romana Sciddurlo's

ALBERO DI PANDORO CON CREMA AL LIMONCELLO

PANDORO CHRISTMAS TREE CAKE WITH LIMONCELLO CREAM

Prep time: 15 minutes
Cook time: 15 minutes
Yield: 8 to 10 servings

If you're looking for a showstopping Christmas dessert, look no further than this Christmas tree cake. *Pandoro* is a classic leavened cake from northern Italy that many Italians enjoy from Christmas to New Year's Day. Its lovely star shape is perfect for layering with some delicate pastry cream that Nonna spikes with limoncello, for a dessert that can double as a gorgeous table centerpiece.

LIMONCELLO CREAM

1¾ cups plus 2 tablespoons (450 ml) whole milk

1¾ cups plus 2 tablespoons (450 ml) limoncello liqueur

½ cup (120 ml) heavy whipping cream

1½ cups (300 g) granulated sugar

¾ cup (90 g) cornstarch

1 teaspoon vanilla extract

10 large egg yolks

Peel of 1 lemon, in 1 long piece

PANDORO

1 store-bought pandoro

1 cup (240 ml) limoncello liqueur

DECORATION

Fresh berries (you can also use candied cherries, if you like), plus more for garnish

Confectioners' sugar, for dusting

1. **To make the limoncello cream:** In a medium saucepan, whisk together the milk, limoncello, heavy cream, granulated sugar, cornstarch, vanilla, egg yolks, and lemon peel until smooth. Turn the heat to medium-low and cook, whisking continuously, until the mixture begins to thicken and bubbles are visible, about 15 minutes. Remove from the heat and continue whisking for 30 more seconds. If necessary, strain through a fine-mesh strainer to remove any lumps. Press plastic wrap directly onto the cream's surface to prevent a skin from forming. Let cool to room temperature.
2. **To make the pandoro:** Lay the pandoro on its side and, using a long serrated knife, cut slices about 2 inches (5 cm) thick. You should be able to get about 5 slices. If the bottom piece is uneven, cut it so it can sit flat.
3. Brush the cut sides of the bottom layer with about one-fifth of the limoncello and top with limoncello cream. Put the next slice on top at an angle so the points of the star are staggered. Repeat with all layers.
4. **To decorate:** Add a fresh berry to each point and dust with confectioners' sugar. Garnish with more fresh berries.

Nonna Angelina Purpura's

DOLCI CON CONFETTINI

ITALIAN SPRINKLE COOKIES

Prep time: 1 hour

Cook time: 30 minutes

Yield: About 48 cookies

The Italian sprinkle cookie has become a cult holiday favorite and Nonna Angelina's are some of the best I've ever had. Her secret is a powdered vanilla extract that comes in packets called Vanillina by the Italian brand Paneangeli ("bread of angels"). Unlike many recipes that require you to cool the cookies completely before glazing, Nonna Angelina glazes them while they're nice and hot, resulting in the sugar drying a pure white color that really makes the sprinkles pop!

COOKIES

4 large eggs, at room temperature

2 packets (½ ounce/15 g each) Italian vanilla powder or 4 teaspoons vanilla extract

1 cup (200 g) granulated sugar

½ cup (1 stick/120 g) unsalted butter, melted

4 teaspoons baking powder

3 cups (360 g) all-purpose or 00 flour

GLAZE

2 cups (240 g) confectioners' sugar

¼ cup (60 ml) whole milk

1 packet (½ ounce/15 g) Italian vanilla powder or 1 teaspoon vanilla extract

1 teaspoon fresh lemon juice or lemon extract (optional)

2 tablespoons unsalted butter, melted

Nonpareils, for decorating

1 **To make the cookies:** In a large bowl, using a handheld electric mixer, beat the eggs, vanilla, and granulated sugar at high speed until pale yellow, about 3 minutes. Add the melted butter and mix at high speed to combine. Add the baking power and mix at low speed to combine. Add the flour, 1 cup (120 g) at a time, and mix at low speed until fully absorbed. Do not overmix. Cover the bowl with plastic wrap and refrigerate for 45 minutes.

2 Preheat the oven to 375°F (190°C). Line a baking sheet with aluminum foil or parchment paper.

3 Roll a tablespoon-size (15 g) chunk of dough between your hands into a 1-inch-thick (2.5 cm) log. Roll the log into a pinwheel and place on the prepared baking sheet. Continue rolling the dough, placing the cookies on the baking sheet 2 inches (5 cm) apart. If the dough feels sticky, chill it in the refrigerator for a few minutes.

4 Bake the cookies until the swirls on the tops have nearly disappeared and the bottoms have slightly browned, 12 to 15 minutes.

5 **Meanwhile make the glaze:** In a small bowl, whisk together the confectioners' sugar, milk, vanilla, and lemon juice (if using). Whisk in the melted butter.

6 Let the cookies cool for 2 minutes. While they are still hot, dip them into the glaze and sprinkle with the nonpareils. Place on a wire rack to cool completely.

Nonna Angelina Says

Don't confuse Vanillina with vanilla-flavored baking powder.

Nonna Antoinette Capodicci's

ROCOCO AL CIOCCOLATO

CHOCOLATE-COVERED ROCOCO

Prep time: 30 minutes
Cook time: 20 minutes
Yield: 12 cookies

Nonna Antoinette is as creative as she is tenacious. One year, she began dreaming up a way to revamp her family's classic *rococo* recipe, which is a yummy spiced cookie from the Campania region—it can fill you with nostalgia, but also leave you needing dental work after eating it. Being the clever Nonna that she is, she added some more dried fruit for softness and covered them in dreamy chocolate for a modern touch. The result is delicious rococo you can't wait to sink your teeth into (pun intended).

ROCOCO

2 cups (290 g) whole almonds, toasted

1 cup (130 to 150 g) dried fruit, such as figs, raisins, or apricots

4 cups (480 g) all-purpose or 00 flour

1 cup (200 g) sugar

¼ cup (80 g) honey

1 tablespoon allspice

2 teaspoons baking powder

1 teaspoon vanilla extract

1 teaspoon orange extract

1 teaspoon lemon extract

Pinch salt

CHOCOLATE DIP

1½ pounds (680 g) bittersweet chocolate chips

1 tablespoon shortening

1. Preheat the oven to 350°F (180°C). Line a baking sheet with parchment paper. Set aside.
2. **To make the rococo:** In a food processor fitted with the blade attachment, process the toasted almonds until finely ground. Add the dried fruit and process until a paste forms. Transfer to the bowl of a stand mixer fitted with the paddle attachment. Mix in the flour, sugar, honey, allspice, baking powder, vanilla extract, orange extract, lemon extract, salt, and ½ cup (120 ml) of water at low speed until well mixed and a hard dough forms.
3. Lightly flour a work surface and turn the dough out onto it. Divide the dough into 12 equal pieces. Roll each piece into a rope 8 inches (20 cm) long and form a bagel-shaped cookie. Place the cookies on the prepared baking sheet about 2 inches (5 cm) apart. Bake for 18 minutes. Transfer to a wire rack to cool.
4. **To make the chocolate dip:** In a double boiler over low heat or in a microwave, melt the chocolate and shortening; stir to combine. Dip each cooled cookie in the melted chocolate until evenly coated. Gently place on a wire rack to cool completely.

Nonna Romana Sciddurlo's

DOLCI S ALLE MANDORLE

GLAZED ALMOND S COOKIES

Prep time: 10 minutes
Cook time: 15 minutes
Yield: About 24 cookies

COOKIES

Nonstick cooking spray, for greasing
4¾ cups (570 g) all-purpose or 00 flour, plus more for dusting
2 teaspoons baking powder
1½ cups (218 g) blanched almonds
6 large eggs, divided
1 cup (200 g) granulated sugar
¾ cup (180 ml) olive oil
Zest of 1 lemon
2 teaspoons vanilla extract
2 tablespoons (30 ml) almond extract

GLAZE

2 cups (240 g) confectioners' sugar
2 tablespoons whole milk
1 tablespoon almond extract
½ teaspoon vanilla extract
Sprinkles, for decorating

Nonna Romana's classic olive-oil S cookies got jazzed up for the holidays, and the result is an impossibly delicious, almond-scented cookie, covered with the dreamiest almond glaze imaginable. When topped with lovely holiday sprinkles, they will be a favorite on your cookie tray.

1. **To make the cookies:** Preheat the oven to 375°F (190°C). Line a baking sheet with aluminum foil or parchment paper. Grease with cooking spray.
2. In a large bowl, whisk together the flour and baking powder.
3. In a food processor, process the almonds for 20 to 30 seconds. Transfer to another large bowl.
4. To the ground almonds, add 5 of the eggs, the granulated sugar, olive oil, lemon zest, and extracts. Using a handheld electric mixer, mix at medium speed until smooth. Add the flour, little by little, mixing at low speed until just absorbed.
5. Lightly flour a work surface and your hands. Take a golf ball–size piece of dough and roll it into a 1-inch-thick (2.5 cm) rope. If the dough is sticky, coat your hands with more flour. Continue making ropes with the remaining dough. Cut the ropes into 4- to 5-inch (10 to 13 cm) pieces and shape each into an S shape. Place the cookies 2 inches (5 cm) apart on the prepared baking sheet. Flatten each cookie slightly with the palm of your hand.
6. In a small bowl, beat the remaining egg. Brush each cookie with the egg wash.
7. Bake until the cookies have browned nicely on the bottom, about 15 minutes. Let cool completely before glazing.
8. **To make the glaze:** In a medium bowl, whisk together the confectioners' sugar, milk, almond extract, and vanilla extract. For a thicker glaze, add more sugar; for a thinner, glaze add more milk. Drizzle the glaze over the cookies and decorate with sprinkles. Let the glaze dry for at least 2 hours.

Nonna Rosetta Rauseo's

PASTATELLE

CHESTNUT CREAM-FILLED COOKIES

Prep time: 1 hour

Cook time: 1 hour 30 minutes

Yield: About 72 cookies

Nonna Rosetta looks forward to Christmas every year so she can make her favorite chestnut cream-filled *pastatelle*. Across the region of Campania, traditional sweets that resemble ravioli are made with a puree of chestnuts or chickpeas mixed with chocolate and stuffed into a lightly sweet dough that is fried until golden brown. Nonna Rosetta prepares these in her kitchen in the most traditional way she was taught back in Aquilonia. When I first asked her to show me how to make these, she warned me: "*Questo e' un procedimento molto lungo!* (This is a long process!)" You can save time by using roasted chestnuts and a pasta roller machine.

FILLING

10 ounces (280 g) roasted chestnuts, peeled

1 ounce (28 g) good-quality semisweet chocolate

2 tablespoons honey

1½ teaspoons unsweetened cocoa powder

Zest of 1 orange

¼ teaspoon ground cinnamon

DOUGH

3 large eggs, beaten

½ cup (100 g) granulated sugar

¼ cup (60 ml) olive oil

Pinch baking powder

2½ cups (300 g) all-purpose or 00 flour, divided, plus more for dusting

Oil, for frying

Confectioners' sugar, for dusting

1. **To make the filling:** In a medium saucepan, combine the chestnuts with enough cold water to cover completely. Place the pan over high heat and bring to a boil. Cook until the chestnuts are tender, 25 to 30 minutes. Using a slotted spoon, transfer the chestnuts to a food processor. Process until smooth. Transfer to a large bowl.
2. In another medium saucepan over low heat, add the chocolate, honey, cocoa powder, orange zest, and cinnamon; cook, stirring occasionally, just until the chocolate melts. Stir in the chestnuts and cook, stirring until very smooth, 3 to 5 minutes. Transfer to a medium bowl and set aside to cool.
3. **To make the dough:** In a large bowl, using a fork, beat the eggs and granulated sugar for 2 minutes. Add the olive oil and mix well. Add the baking powder and mix well. Add 2 cups (240 g) of the flour. Mix until all the flour is absorbed and a dough begins to form.
4. Generously flour a work surface and turn the dough out onto it. Add the remaining ½ cup (60 g) flour, kneading it in by hand until the dough is smooth and supple, 5 to 7 minutes. Cover the dough with plastic wrap and let rest for 10 minutes.
5. Using a pasta roller on a #3 setting, begin passing the dough through until no holes remain and you have a sheet about 3 inches (7.5 cm) wide. Lay the dough sheet on a work surface.

CONTINUED ON PAGE 182

CONTINUED FROM PAGE 181

6 Dot teaspoons of filling down one side of the dough, about 1½ inches (4 cm) apart, leaving a border of at least ½ inch (12 mm) on all sides. Fold the dough over to cover the filling. Press down on the edge of the dough and press the areas around the filling together to create pockets that resemble ravioli. Cut out squares with a ravioli cutter and seal. Place the filled dough squares on a clean kitchen towel, making sure they do not touch one another. You can fry or bake these cookies.

7 **To fry:** Line a plate with paper towels. In a small stockpot, heat about 2 inches (5 cm) of oil over high heat. Working in batches, fry the cookies until golden brown, 2 to 3 minutes per batch. Transfer to the prepared plate.

8 **To bake:** Preheat the oven to 375°F (190°C). Place the pastatelle on an ungreased baking sheet 1 inch (2.5 cm) apart. Bake until lightly golden, 15 to 18 minutes.

9 Dust with confectioners' sugar while warm.

Nonna Cecilia Debellis'

DOLCI TRICOLORE

SEVEN-LAYER COOKIES

Prep time: 2 hours 15 minutes
Cook time: 12 minutes
Yield: Several dozen

I don't think I've ever met a person who didn't like seven-layer cookies, also called rainbow cookies. Nonna Cecilia learned to make this Italian-American classic cookie from her Commara Maria, who had come to America before her, and it quickly made its way into her repertoire.

- 4 large eggs, separated, whites beaten until foamy
- 1 cup (2 sticks/240 g) unsalted butter, at room temperature
- 1 cup (200 g) sugar
- 12 ounces (340 g) almond paste, broken into small chunks
- 2 cups (240 ml) all-purpose or 00 flour
- Red and green food coloring
- ½ cup (160 g) apricot jam
- 4 ounces (113 g) good-quality semisweet chocolate

1. Preheat the oven to 375°F (190°C).
2. In the bowl of a stand mixer fitted with the paddle attachment, mix the egg yolks and butter at medium speed until combined. Add the sugar and mix until incorporated. Add the almond paste and mix at medium speed until smooth. Reduce the speed to low and add the flour, a little at a time. Add the egg whites and mix at low speed until a soft, uniform dough forms.
3. Divide the dough into 3 equal parts and place them in 3 separate bowls. Leave one of the parts of dough the natural white color. Add as much of the red food coloring to one bowl, and the green food coloring to the other to achieve your desired shades.
4. Spread the dough into 3 separate 8 by 12-inch (20 by 30 cm) baking pans. Bake for 10 to 12 minutes and let cool completely.
5. Line a clean work surface with parchment paper. Flip the green cookie layer out of the baking sheet onto the parchment. Spread half the apricot jam over the green layer and top it with the white cookie layer and spread the remaining apricot jam in an even layer. Place the red cookie layer on top and press the sheets firmly together with your hands.
6. With a serrated knife, trim all 4 edges to even them out.
7. In a double boiler or microwave, melt the chocolate, then spread it over the top. Refrigerate until the chocolate is set, about 1 hour, or preferably overnight.
8. Flip the layers so the chocolate side is facing the parchment paper and coat the bottom with melted chocolate. Refrigerate until the chocolate is set, about 1 hour. Cut into 1½ by ½-inch (4 by 1.5 cm) cookies and serve.

Nonna Romana Sciddurlo's

DOLCI AL CANNOLO

CANNOLI COOKIES

Prep time: 20 minutes
Cook time: 12 minutes
Yield: About 48 cookies

I didn't think it was possible to get all the flavors of a cannoli in a single cookie, but guess what? It is! Nonna Romana and I jazzed up her classic ricotta cookie recipe with notes of orange and cinnamon, before adding some yummy pistachios and chocolate chips to the batter for crunch and texture. I love decorating these with a gorgeous, thick white glaze and different-colored candied cherries to put everyone in the holiday mood.

COOKIES

1 cup (125 g) unsalted pistachios
2 cups (240 g) all-purpose or 00 flour
1½ teaspoons baking powder
½ teaspoon salt
1 cup (200 g) granulated sugar
½ cup (1 stick/120 g) unsalted butter, at room temperature
2 teaspoons vanilla extract
1¼ teaspoons ground cinnamon
Zest of 1 orange
1 large egg, at room temperature
8 ounces (225 g) whole-milk ricotta, at room temperature
1 cup (180 g) mini semisweet chocolate chips

GLAZE

2 cups (240 g) confectioners' sugar
3 tablespoons milk, plus more as needed
¼ teaspoon vanilla extract

DECORATING

Crushed pistachios
Candied cherries

1. **To make the cookies:** Preheat the oven to 350°F (180°C). Line a baking sheet with parchment paper.
2. In a food processor fitted with the blade attachment, process the pistachios until coarsely chopped, 15 to 20 seconds. Transfer to a small bowl.
3. In a large bowl, whisk together the flour, baking powder, and salt.
4. In the bowl of a stand mixer fitted with the paddle attachment, beat the granulated sugar, butter, vanilla, cinnamon, and orange zest at medium-high speed until fluffy, about 5 minutes. Add the egg and ricotta; mix at medium-high speed to combine. Add the dry ingredients, little by little, and mix at medium-high speed until a dough forms. Mix in the pistachios and chocolate chips.
5. Roll tablespoons of the dough balls, and place them 2 inches (5 cm) apart on the prepared baking sheet.
6. Bake until bottoms are slightly brown, 10 to 12 minutes. Let cool completely before glazing.
7. **To make the glaze:** In a medium bowl, whisk together the confectioners' sugar, milk, and vanilla until a smooth glaze forms. Add less milk for a thicker glaze or more for a thinner glaze. Spoon the glaze over the cookies and decorate with chopped pistachios and candied cherries as desired.

SAINTS' DAYS

CELEBRATIONS

SAINT LUCY'S DAY (DECEMBER 13)

CELEBRATIONS

Nonna Romana Sciddurlo's

CARBONE DELLA BEFANA

SWEET COAL

Prep time: 3 hours
Cook time: 20 minutes
Yield: About 12 pieces of coal

In an Italian household, Epiphany officially marks the end of the Christmas season. Ever since I was a little girl, Nonna Romana would tell me stories of the good witch La Befana, who would visit children on the eve of January 6 to give the good little boys and girls gifts of candy and treats, while anyone who misbehaved (you can guess which list I was usually on) received coal. She would recite the famous Befana poem to me until I knew it by heart: "*La Befana viene di notte, con le scarpe tutte rotte, il vestito alla Romana, viva viva la Befana!*" When I woke one Epiphany morning many years ago and walked over to the fireplace to see what La Befana had left me, to my shock and surprise, it looked like there were lumps of coal in a dish! Upon further inspection, I found that it wasn't coal at all, but candy that looked exactly like the real thing—my father, Vito, had teamed up with Nonna Romana to trick me. This recipe is perfect for your little ones who are a little naughty, a little nice, and very sweet.

1 large egg white
¾ cup (150 g) plus 1⅓ cups (265 g) granulated sugar, divided
1 tablespoon vodka
2 teaspoons fresh lemon juice
¾ cup (90 g) confectioners' sugar
3 or 4 drops black food coloring

1. Line a loaf pan with parchment paper.
2. In a large bowl, using a handheld electric mixer, beat the egg white at high speed until stiff peaks form. Add ¾ cup (150 g) of the granulated sugar, the vodka, and the lemon juice, and mix at medium-high speed. Add the confectioners' sugar and food coloring, and mix at medium-high speed until a thick icing forms.
3. In a small heavy-bottomed saucepan, bring 2 cups (480 ml) of water and the remaining 1⅓ cups (265 g) granulated sugar to a boil over high heat, then reduce the heat to medium-low and cook until the sugar reaches a light caramel color.
4. Add the icing, stirring constantly until well combined.
5. Transfer the mixture to the prepared loaf pan and let rest at room temperature until hardened, about 3 hours or overnight.
6. Turn it out of the pan and break into irregularly shaped pieces that resemble coal.

Nonna Liliana Barone's

BUCATINI CON LE SARDE

BUCATINI WITH SARDINES

Prep time: 30 minutes
Cook time: 40 minutes
Yield: 4 to 6 servings

Every Sicilian family has their own recipe for *pasta con sarde*, which they hold dear to their hearts, but Nonna Liliana stole my heart with her incredible recipe for this iconic Saint Joseph's Day pasta dish. The typical preparation involves a combination of wild fennel, or *finocchietto selvatico*; fresh sardines, which have to be cleaned and deboned, one by one; and a mix of pine nuts and tomato concentrate, all tossed over saffron yellow-tinted bucatini pasta. While *bucatini con le sarde* seems exotic by today's standards, it's important to remember that it is part of Italy's *cucina povera* (peasant food) and utilizes ingredients that were quite abundant in the Sicilian landscape. If you have a hard time finding the wild fennel, regular fennel is an adequate substitute, although milder in flavor.

- 2 pounds (910 g) fresh sardines
- ¼ cup (38 g) currants
- 1 cup (240 ml) warm water
- 6 tablespoons extra-virgin olive oil, divided
- ½ cup (55 g) plain bread crumbs
- ¼ cup (22 g) fennel stems, cut into ¼-inch (6 mm) dice
- 2 tablespoons salt, plus more to taste
- 5 ounces (140 g) fresh wild fennel fronds or regular fennel if you cannot find wild fennel
- 1 large onion, cut into ¼-inch (6 mm) dice
- ¼ cup (34 g) pignoli (pine nuts)
- 1 tablespoon tomato concentrate or tomato paste
- 0.016 ounce (0.5 g) saffron threads (about 2 packets), divided
- ¼ cup (37 g) sardines or anchovies packed in salt (about 4 fish)
- 16 ounces (455 g) dried bucatini pasta

1. Rinse the fresh sardines under cold running water. On a clean work surface, using a sharp paring knife, remove the heads and the dorsal fins, and scrape the bodies to remove the scales. Rinse under cold running water to remove any remaining loose scales. Beginning at the point where the tail meets the body, slice open the belly of the sardines, scrape out the entrails with your knife, and discard. Fillet the fish in half, remove the center bone, and discard.
2. In a small bowl, combine the currants with the warm water to rehydrate. Let soak while you continue with the recipe.
3. In a medium skillet over medium heat, combine 2 tablespoons of the olive oil and the bread crumbs. Cook, stirring constantly, until the bread crumbs just begin to turn lightly golden, 5 to 7 minutes. Remove from the heat and immediately transfer to a medium bowl.
4. In a large stockpot, bring the fennel stems, 4 quarts (3.8 L) of water, and 2 tablespoons (30 ml) salt to a boil over high heat.
5. Fill a small stockpot halfway with water and bring it to a boil over high heat. Add the fennel fronds and cook, uncovered, for 10 minutes. With a slotted spoon, transfer the fronds to a small bowl. Reserve the cooking water.

CONTINUED ON PAGE 192

CONTINUED FROM PAGE 190

6 In a large skillet, heat the remaining 4 tablespoons olive oil over medium heat. Add the onion and cook, stirring occasionally, until soft and translucent, 5 to 7 minutes. Add the pignoli and cook, stirring occasionally, until toasted, 2 to 3 minutes. Drain and add the currants; discard the soaking water. Stir in the tomato concentrate and 1 cup (240 ml) of the reserved fennel-frond cooking water.

7 Coarsely chop the fennel fronds. Add them to the skillet along with another 1 cup (240 ml) of the reserved fennel-frond cooking water.

8 In a small cup, stir together half of the saffron threads with 2 tablespoons (30 ml) of the reserved fennel-frond cooking water and add it to the skillet. Cook for 1 minute. Add the fresh sardines and the salt-packed sardines, along with another ¼ cup (60 ml) of the reserved fennel-frond cooking water. Cook until the flesh is just firm, 4 to 5 minutes. Do not overcook. If the pan looks dry, add enough of the reserved fennel-frond cooking water so it just slightly pools at the bottom of the pan. Season with salt to taste. Remove from the heat.

9 Drop the pasta into the boiling water with the fennel stems and cook until al dente.

10 In a small cup, stir together the remaining half of the saffron threads with 2 tablespoons of the pasta cooking water and add it to the pot with the pasta. Scoop out the cooked pasta and add it to the sardine mixture. Turn the heat to medium and cook, tossing, for 1 to 2 minutes.

11 Transfer to a serving dish and top with the sautéed bread crumbs. Serve immediately.

Nonna Liliana Says

Domani è più buono di oggi! (This is one of those dishes that is even better the next day!) We all look forward to San Giuseppe so we can enjoy this dish for two straight days, because it's that good!

Nonna Lydia Palermo's

SFINCI E ZEPPOLE DI SAN GIUSEPPE

SAINT JOSEPH SFINCI AND ZEPPOLE

Prep time: 1 hour

Cook time: 45 minutes

Yield: 14 sfinci or 8 zeppole

Italians and Italian-Americans rejoice in the weeks leading up to Saint Joseph's Day, as bakeries begin to stock *zeppole* and *sfinci* galore. Nonna Lydia's recipe is from her brother's bakery in Queens, and he learned it from his Sicilian Mamma. Many would line up early in the morning on Saint Joseph's Day in hopes of getting a warm pastry to start the day Italian-style. The classic zeppole is a piped choux dough that can be baked or fried and filled with Pastry Cream (page 6); sfinci, their Sicilian cousins, can only be fried and are filled with sweetened Cannoli Cream (page 7). If the pressure of choosing between team zeppole and team sfinci is too much to handle, Nonna Lydia has a solution: "Have one of each!"

DOUGH

¼ cup (50 g) shortening

Pinch salt

1 cup (120 g) all-purpose or 00 flour

4 large eggs

Oil, for frying and dipping

SFINCI FILLING AND DECORATION

1 Cannoli Cream recipe (page 7)

14 pieces candied orange peel

14 candied cherries

Crushed pistachios, for sprinkling

ZEPPOLE FILLING AND DECORATION

1 Pastry Cream recipe (page 6)

8 Amarena cherries

Confectioners' sugar, for dusting

1. **To make the dough:** In a medium saucepan, bring 1 cup (240 ml) of water, the shortening, and salt to a boil over high heat. Add the flour, reduce the heat to low, and mix with a wooden spoon, continuously, until all the flour is incorporated and a soft dough that pulls away from the sides of the pan forms, about 30 seconds. Turn off the heat and continue stirring for 30 seconds more. Remove from the heat and transfer the dough to a medium bowl. Let cool.
2. When cool enough to handle, mix the dough with your hands for 5 minutes. If you find any clumps of flour that did not dissolve, remove and discard them. Let cool to room temperature.
3. Add 1 egg, mixing with your hands until completely absorbed. Repeat with the second egg. Add the third egg and, using a handheld electric mixer, mix at medium speed until the egg is fully absorbed. Repeat with the remaining egg and mixing until the dough is very smooth.
4. **If making sfinci:** Line a plate with paper towels. In a small stockpot, heat about 2½ inches (6 cm) of oil over high heat. Use a thermometer to maintain the temperature between 375° and 400°F (190° and 200°C).

CONTINUED ON PAGE 195

CONTINUED FROM PAGE 193

5 Fill a small bowl with olive oil. Using a small ice cream scoop or a spoon, and working in batches of 3, dip the scoop in the olive oil, scoop the dough, and carefully drop the dough into the hot oil. Fry until golden brown and they no longer pop and expand, about 5 minutes. With a slotted spoon, transfer to the prepared plate. Let cool before slicing and filling. The sfinci will be hollow on the inside.

6 Slice the sfinci three-quarters of the way through and fill with about 2 tablespoons of cannoli cream. Top each sfinci with a candied orange peel, a candied cherry, and crushed pistachios.

7 **If frying zeppole:** Cut out eight 4-inch (10 cm) squares of parchment paper.

8 Fill a disposable pastry bag, fitted with a large star tip, with the dough. Carefully pipe a 3-inch (7.5 cm) circle of dough onto each piece of parchment. Overlap the dough by no more than 1 inch (2.5 cm).

9 Line a plate with paper towels. In a small stockpot, heat about 2½ inches (6 cm) of oil over high heat. Use a thermometer to maintain the temperature between 375° and 400°F (190° and 200°C). Working in batches of 3, carefully drop pieces of parchment paper with the dough circles attached into the hot oil. Using tongs, remove the parchment paper from the oil. Fry the zeppole until golden brown, about 5 minutes per batch. With a slotted spoon, transfer to the prepared plate. Let cool completely before slicing and filling.

10 **If baking zeppole:** Preheat the oven to 425°F (220°C). Line a baking sheet with parchment paper. Carefully pipe eight 3-inch (7.5 cm) circles of dough onto the prepared baking sheet, spacing them about 2 inches (5 cm) apart. Overlap the dough by no more than 1 inch (2.5 cm). Bake until golden, 18 to 20 minutes. Let cool completely before slicing and filling.

11 **Fill the zeppole:** Slice the zeppole in half horizontally. Using a a disposable pastry bag fitted with a star tip, pipe the cream onto the bottom half and top with the other half. Pipe a bit of cream in the center and top with an Amarena cherry. Dust with confectioners' sugar.

Nonna Rosa Vella's

FRITTELLE DI SAN GIUSEPPE

TUSCAN RICE FRITTERS

Prep time: 1 hour 30 minutes
Cook time: 1 hour
Yield: About 48 fritters

The first time I ever met Nonna Rosa, she was frying these fritters on her stove in her kitchen and her whole house smelled like heaven! These *frittelle* are prepared in Tuscany and most of central Italy to celebrate Saint Joseph's Day on March 19, but Nonna Rosa doesn't need a calendar to tell her when to make something: "To tell the truth, I make all the time because everybody love-a!" These fritters are crispy on the outside and have soft, citrus-scented rice on the inside that takes on an almost creamy texture. Try your best, but it will be very hard to have just one!

RICE

2 cups (480 ml) whole milk

1 small navel orange, quartered

½ lemon, quartered

2 cups (370 g) long-grain rice

1¼ cups (250 g) sugar

FRITTERS

3 large eggs

2 large egg yolks

Zest of 1 orange

Zest of 1 lemon

1 packet (½ ounce/15 g) Italian vanilla powder or 2 teaspoons vanilla extract

¼ cup (60 ml) Vin Santo

¼ cup (30 g) all-purpose or 00 flour

1½ teaspoons baking powder

Olive oil, for frying

1. **To make the rice:** In a medium saucepan, bring the milk, 2 cups (480 ml) of water, orange, and lemon to a boil over medium-high heat. Do not worry if the milk begins to separate a little. Drop in the rice, reduce the heat to low, and cook, uncovered, for 10 minutes. Stir in the sugar and cook, uncovered, until the rice is tender but still has some bite, 10 to 15 minutes. Remove from the heat. Remove and discard the lemon and orange.
2. Transfer the rice to a shallow baking dish and spread it into an even layer. Cover with a clean kitchen towel and let cool for 1 hour.
3. **To make the fritters:** In a large bowl, stir together the cooled rice, the eggs, egg yolks, orange zest, lemon zest, vanilla, and Vin Santo until well combined. Add the flour and baking powder and stir until just combined.
4. Line a plate with paper towels. In a large heavy-bottomed skillet, heat about 1 inch (2.5 cm) of olive oil over high heat.
5. Working in batches, with a small ice cream scoop, carefully drop scoops of the rice into the hot oil. Flatten each scoop with the back of a spoon. Fry until very golden brown, about 3 minutes per side. With a slotted spoon, transfer to the prepared plate. Serve hot or warm.

Nonna Angelina Purpura's

MINESTRA DI SAN GIUSEPPE

SAINT JOSEPH'S DAY MINESTRONE

Prep time: 20 minutes
Cook time: 1 hour 5 minutes
Yield: 8 to 10 servings

Saint Joseph's Day in Sicily is a day of great celebration, but to many Sicilians, it is also a day to give back. Nonna Angelina's flavorful minestrone is traditionally made to mark the holiday and perform an act of charity. Nonna Angelina recalls that many families in Sicily who felt they had been blessed by Saint Joseph would prepare large pots of this vegetable stew to give to the less fortunate. The traditional *minestra* would be made with any seasonal vegetables and legumes they could find at home or growing in nearby fields. It's very easy to make, and a beautiful example of Sicily's *cucina povera* (peasant food).

1 teaspoon salt, plus more for cooking the vegetables

10 ounces (280 g) broccoli florets

½ head escarole, washed and cut into 1-inch (2.5 cm) strips

1 bunch chicory, washed and cut into 2-inch (5 cm) pieces

1 bunch red Swiss chard, washed, ends trimmed, and cut into 2-inch (5 cm) pieces

3 tablespoons extra-virgin olive oil

3 cloves garlic, sliced

1 small onion, cut into ¼-inch (6 mm) dice

1 cup (149 g) cherry tomatoes, halved

¼ teaspoon black pepper

4 or 5 fresh basil leaves

1 can (15 ounces/425 g) chickpeas, drained and rinsed

1 can (15 ounces/425 g) lentils, drained and rinsed

1 can (15 ounces/425 g) cannellini beans, drained and rinsed

1½ cups (360 ml) vegetable broth

1. Bring a large stockpot of lightly salted water to a boil over high heat. Drop in the broccoli and boil until tender, 7 to 10 minutes. With a large slotted spoon or tongs, transfer the broccoli to a large bowl. Bring the water back to a boil. Drop in the escarole and boil until tender, 12 to 15 minutes; transfer to the bowl with the broccoli. Bring the water back to a boil. Add the chicory and red Swiss chard and boil until tender, 17 to 20 minutes; transfer to the bowl with the other vegetables.
2. Heat a small stockpot over medium heat and add the olive oil, garlic, and onion. Cook, stirring occasionally, until the onion is translucent, 5 to 7 minutes. Add the cherry tomatoes, 1 teaspoon salt, pepper, and basil. Cook, stirring occasionally, for 2 minutes. Add the chickpeas, lentils, cannellini beans, and broth and bring to a boil over medium-high heat; cook until heated through, 7 to 10 minutes. Transfer the vegetables to a casserole dish, top with the legume mixture and mix well.
3. Serve in warm bowls with some crusty semolina bread, if desired.

Nonna Romana Sciddurlo's

LAGANE DI SAN GIUSEPPE

MAFALDINE PASTA WITH ANCHOVIES

Prep time: 5 minutes
Cook time: 15 minutes
Yield: 4 to 6 servings

Lagane di San Giuseppe is the traditional Pugliese dish only prepared for Saint Joseph's Day, and the ingredients are selected to honor Saint Joseph's profession as a carpenter. The *mafaldine*, which look like tiny lasagna noodles, represent curled wood shavings, while the toasted bread crumbs evoke sawdust. This dish is very simple but requires excellent timing, as adding water to hot oil and anchovies can be a bit explosive, but the aromatic pasta comes together quickly and is delicious when topped with the toasted bread crumbs. You'll want to make it more than once a year!

1 cup (108 g) plain bread crumbs
3 tablespoons (45 ml) plus ½ cup (120 ml) extra-virgin olive oil, divided
Salt
16 ounces (455 g) dried mafaldine
1 can (2 ounces, or 56 g) anchovies, drained and broken into small pieces

1. Heat a large high-sided skillet over medium heat. Add the bread crumbs and 3 tablespoons of the olive oil to the pan and cook, stirring constantly, until the bread crumbs just begin to turn lightly golden, 5 to 7 minutes. Remove from the heat and immediately transfer to a medium bowl to prevent burning. (Bread crumbs will continue to cook if left in the pan.)
2. Bring a medium stockpot of generously salted water to a boil over high heat. Drop in the pasta and cook according to the package instructions.
3. When the pasta has 2 to 3 minutes to go before it is al dente, heat the remaining ½ cup (120 ml) olive oil in a medium saucepan over medium-high heat. Once the oil is very hot, add the anchovies and stir carefully with a wooden spoon for about 5 seconds. (There may be some splatters, but it will calm down when you add the water.) Scoop out about 1 cup (240 ml) of the pasta water and add it to the skillet, stirring until the anchovies have dissolved.
4. Drain the pasta and transfer it to a large serving bowl. Add the anchovy mixture and toss well to coat the pasta. Sprinkle with the toasted bread crumbs, reserving some for garnish. Serve the pasta in warm bowls and garnish with some extra bread crumbs on top.

Nonna Romana Says

The trick to this recipe is not letting the anchovies cook too much before adding the water. As soon as they begin to break apart, be ready with the ladle.

Nonna Romana Sciddurlo's

ROSETTE DI SAN GIUSEPPE

SAINT JOSEPH BREAD ROLLS

Prep time: 1 hour 30 minutes
Cook time: 25 minutes
Yield: 22 rolls

Many Italians in America have maintained the beautiful tradition of making an altar to honor Saint Joseph, the patron saint of Sicily. The first altars were created to give thanks for a rainstorm after a very long drought, which had caused intense famine throughout Sicily. As the rain fell and nourished the people, they began to make altars full of food to show their gratitude to Saint Joseph. Over the years, the altars have become more and more ornate, involving breads made into intricate shapes, like staves and chalices.

- ⅔ cup (160 ml) whole milk
- 1 packet (¼ ounce/7 g) active dry yeast
- 2¾ cups (385 g) bread flour, divided
- ¼ cup (50 g) sugar
- 1 teaspoon salt
- 2 tablespoons lard, melted
- 3 large eggs, divided
- 2 teaspoons anise extract
- Extra-virgin olive oil, for brushing
- Sesame seeds, for sprinkling

1. In a small saucepan over medium heat, heat the milk until warm but not hot. Transfer to the bowl of a stand mixer fitted with the dough hook attachment. Add the yeast and let stand for 10 minutes.
2. Add 1 cup (140 g) of the flour, the sugar, salt, and melted lard; mix at low speed until the flour is absorbed. Add 2 of the eggs, the anise extract, and another cup (140 g) of the flour; mix at low speed until the flour is absorbed. Add the remaining ¾ cup (105 g) flour and mix at low speed until the flour is mostly absorbed and a ball of dough begins to form.
3. Turn the dough out onto a clean work surface and knead with your hands until all of the flour is absorbed and the dough is smooth and supple, about 5 minutes. Brush a large bowl with olive oil and place the dough in it. Flip the dough to coat it in the oil. Cover the bowl with plastic wrap and let rest in a warm place for 1 hour.
4. Preheat the oven to 350°F (180°C). Line a baking sheet with parchment paper.
5. Punch down the dough and knead it for 2 to 3 minutes. Take a chunk of dough and roll it into a rope about 8 inches (20 cm) long and 1 inch (2.5 cm) thick. With a knife, make cuts about halfway through the rope, ½ inch (12 mm) apart. Roll the rope into a pinwheel and pinch the ends together to form a rose shape. Place on the prepared baking sheet. Repeat with the remaining dough.
6. In a small bowl, beat the remaining egg with a fork. Brush the rolls with the egg wash and sprinkle with sesame seeds. Bake until golden brown, 20 to 25 minutes.

Nonna Antoinette Capodicci's

FRESE DI SAN ROCCO

BREAD OF SAINT ROCCO

Prep time: 3 hours 3 minutes
Cook time: 20 minutes
Yield: 3 frese

In Nonna Antoinette's hometown of Morcone, just outside Naples, this traditional bread is baked to honor Saint Rocco. These loaves would be baked a few days before the holiday, so they could dry out a bit. On the feast day of Saint Rocco (August 16), they would be taken into the country for a picnic by a natural spring. According to tradition, using the spring water to moisten your *frese* could bring you good fortune.

- 1 packet (¼ ounce/7 g) active dry yeast
- 1¼ cups (300 ml) warm water, divided
- 4 large eggs, at room temperature, divided
- 2 ounces (55 g) lard, at room temperature
- ¼ cup (60 ml) extra-virgin olive oil, plus more for brushing and greasing
- 4 cups (560) bread flour, plus more for dusting
- 2 teaspoons salt
- ¼ teaspoon black pepper

1. In the bowl of a stand mixer fitted with the dough hook attachment, dissolve the yeast in 1 cup (240 ml) of the warm water. Let stand until the mixture bubbles, about 3 minutes.
2. Add 3 of the eggs and the lard and mix at low speed to combine. With the mixer running at low speed, stream in the olive oil. Gradually, add the flour, and continue mixing until incorporated. Add the salt, pepper, and the remaining ¼ cup (60 ml) warm water. Increase the speed to medium and mix until a smooth, supple dough that no longer sticks to the sides of the bowl forms. The dough should be very wet but not stick to your hands.
3. Brush a large bowl with olive oil and place the dough inside the bowl. Cover the bowl with plastic wrap and let rest in a warm place until the dough has doubled in size, about 1 hour and 30 minutes to 2 hours.
4. Grease two baking sheets with olive oil.
5. Lightly flour a work surface and turn the dough out onto it. Divide the dough into 3 equal pieces. Roll each piece into a 2-inch-thick (5 cm) rope and shape each rope into a ring. Arrange the rings on the prepared baking sheets, making sure they don't touch. Cover the baking sheets with a clean kitchen towel and let rest in a warm place until the dough has doubled in size, about 1 hour.
6. Preheat the oven to 400°F (200°C).
7. In a small bowl, beat the remaining egg. Brush the top of each ring with the beaten egg and bake until golden brown, 18 to 20 minutes.

Nonna Carmela Tornatore's

UOVA IN PURGATORIO CON POLENTA

EGGS IN PURGATORY WITH POLENTA

Prep time: 15 minutes
Cook time: 30 minutes
Yield: 4 servings

It is said that on All Souls' Day we also honor our faithfully departed souls who are in purgatory. This recipe consists of eggs cooked in a fiery tomato sauce that will awaken your taste buds and feed your soul. Leave it to Italians to make suffering into an excuse to eat a delicious meal!

EGGS IN PURGATORY

3 tablespoons extra-virgin olive oil

½ teaspoon red pepper flakes (optional)

¼ teaspoon black pepper

1 small onion, cut into ½-inch (13 mm) dice

½ medium green bell pepper, cut into ½-inch (13 mm) dice

2 cloves garlic, sliced

1 can (14 ounces/400 g) crushed tomatoes

½ teaspoon salt

4 large eggs

1 tablespoon chopped fresh basil

POLENTA

¼ cup (60 ml) whole milk

1 chicken bouillon cube

Salt

1 cup (140 g) quick-cooking polenta

2 tablespoons unsalted butter

Black pepper

1. **To make the eggs in purgatory:** Heat a large skillet with a lid over medium heat. Add the olive oil, red pepper flakes (if using), black pepper, onion, bell pepper, and garlic and cook, stirring occasionally, for 2 to 3 minutes. Reduce the heat to low and cook, stirring occasionally, until the onion softens, 5 to 7 minutes. Add the tomatoes and salt and bring the mixture to a boil over medium-high heat. Reduce the heat to low, cover the pan, and simmer for 10 minutes.
2. **Meanwhile, make the polenta:** In a large saucepan, bring 3 cups (720 ml) of water, the milk, and the bouillon cube to a boil over high heat. Season with salt to taste. Gradually stream in the polenta while whisking constantly to avoid clumps. Reduce the heat to low and simmer, stirring occasionally, for 2 to 3 minutes. Whisk in the butter.
3. **To finish the eggs in purgatory:** Carefully crack each egg into a separate small bowl, ramekin, or even an espresso cup.
4. Increase the heat under the sauce to medium. Make 4 small wells, in the sauce with a wooden spoon and fill each well with an egg. Sprinkle the eggs with the basil, cover the pan, and cook until the egg whites are white and the yolks are firm, 2 to 3 minutes. Cook for less time if you like your eggs a bit runnier. Season with pepper and serve the eggs and sauce over the warm polenta.

Nonna Teresa Petruccelli-Formato's

SCAROLA RIPIENA

STUFFED ESCAROLE

Prep time: 20 minutes
Cook time: 1 hour
Yield: 4 servings

Roman-born Nonna Teresa learned this recipe that honors All Souls' Day from her Neapolitan mother-in-law. "My wonderful mother-in-law would say that stuffing the escarole and wrapping it up represented our loved ones' eternal rest." She warns not to remove the base of the escarole, which will make tying the leaves down with kitchen twine difficult.

2 small heads escarole, washed
2 to 3 slices day-old bread
1 cup (155 g) Kalamata or Gaeta olives, pitted and halved
2 teaspoons capers
⅔ cup (67 g) grated Parmigiano-Reggiano cheese
⅔ cup (77 g) plain bread crumbs
½ cup (68 g) pignoli (pine nuts)
¼ cup (16 g) minced fresh parsley
2 large eggs, beaten
¼ cup (35 g) raisins
5 anchovy fillets packed in oil, broken up into little pieces
3 tablespoons extra-virgin olive oil
3 cloves garlic, sliced
1⅓ cups (320 ml) chicken broth

1. Remove any brown outer leaves from each head of escarole head and trim about ¼ inch (6 mm) off the bottom—you want to trim away any brown. Pull the leaves open and cut out the 2-inch-wide (5 cm) center bulb in each head, leaving only the large outer leaves. This will make room for the filling. Pat the escarole dry.
2. In a small bowl, combine the day-old bread with enough cold water to cover it and let soak for 2 minutes. Squeeze out the excess moisture from the bread and discard the water.
3. To a large bowl, add the bread, olives, capers, cheese, bread crumbs, pignoli, parsley, eggs, raisins, and anchovies and stir until well combined and the mixture holds its shape. Divide the filling in half and place it in the center of each escarole head, but do not spread it out.
4. Holding all the leaves of an escarole head together tightly with one hand, wrap kitchen twine around it, from the base up, and tie it together. Repeat with the second head.
5. In a large skillet with a lid, heat the olive oil over medium heat. Add the garlic and cook, stirring occasionally, for 1 minute. Add the stuffed escarole and cover the skillet; cook until the escarole begins to wilt, about 3 minutes. Using tongs, turn the escarole. Reduce the heat to low, cover, and cook for 15 minutes.
6. Add the chicken broth to the skillet and increase the heat to medium; cover, and bring to a boil. Cook until the escarole has wilted to half its size and the broth has reduced by half, about 15 minutes. Uncover and turn the escarole once more. Cook, uncovered, for 15 minutes.
7. Remove the twine from the escarole, cut each head in half, and serve.

Nonna Anna Buonsante's

MINESTRA DEI MORTI

BUTTERNUT SQUASH WITH POTATOES AND FAVA BEANS

Prep time: 1 hour, plus 24 hours soaking

Cook time: 45 minutes

Yield: 4 to 6 servings

In Nonna Anna's hometown of Mola di Bari, this hearty minestrone with autumnal flavors was made to commemorate the dead on All Souls' Day. The sweetness of the butternut squash mingles beautifully with the fried onions, while the skin of the fava beans adds wonderful texture to this dish. It's perfect for an evening when there's a little chill in the air.

16 ounces (455 g) dried fava beans

2 pounds (910 g) Yukon Gold potatoes (about 7 small potatoes), scrubbed, peeled, and cut into 1-inch (2.5 cm) chunks

1 pound (455 g) butternut squash, peeled and cut into 1-inch (2.5 cm) chunks

½ cup (120 ml) plus 5 tablespoons extra-virgin olive oil, divided

2 teaspoons salt

5 cups (1.2 L) boiling water

1 medium onion, sliced

1. In a large saucepan, combine the dried fava beans with enough cold water to cover completely. Cover the pan with plastic wrap and let the beans soak for 24 hours.
2. Drain the beans. Using a small knife or your fingernail, peel the black line off each fava bean. Do not peel off all the skin. Transfer to a medium bowl.
3. Heat a large skillet with a lid over medium-high heat. Add the fava beans, potatoes, butternut squash, 5 tablespoons of the olive oil, and the salt. Cook, stirring frequently, for 5 to 7 minutes. Add the boiling water so that it just barely covers everything. Reduce the heat to medium, cover the pan, and cook until the fava beans begin to break down and the potatoes and butternut squash are tender, 25 to 30 minutes.
4. In another large skillet, heat the remaining ½ cup (120 ml) oil over medium heat. Add the onion and cook, stirring occasionally, until the edges of the onion just begin to turn golden brown, 6 to 7 minutes. Remove from the heat and transfer to the skillet with the fava beans, potatoes, and butternut squash, and gently stir to combine. Serve in warm bowls with some crusty Italian bread, if desired.

Nonna Chiara Tapino's

LE DITA DELLA STREGA

WITCH FINGER COOKIES

Prep time: 1 hour 15 minutes
Cook time: 15 minutes
Yield: About 24 cookies

They began celebrating Halloween in Italy a few years ago, and while it's not quite the same as Halloween in America, they've created a few themed treats to get into the spirit of things. These deliciously spooky almond shortbread cookies are made to look like real witch fingers! The strawberry jam enables the whole-almond nails to stick to the cookies and gives them a ghoulish feel that all the kids will love!

- 1½ ounces (43 g) slivered almonds
- ½ cup (1 stick/120 g) unsalted butter, at room temperature
- ⅓ cup (40 g) confectioners' sugar
- 1 large egg yolk
- ½ teaspoon almond extract
- 1½ cups (180 g) all-purpose or 00 flour
- ½ teaspoon baking powder
- 24 whole almonds
- Strawberry jam, for brushing

1. In a food processor fitted with the knife blade, process the slivered almonds until fine, 40 to 60 seconds. Transfer to the bowl of a stand mixer fitted with the paddle attachment.
2. Add the butter, confectioners' sugar, egg yolk, and almond extract; mix at medium speed until combined. Add the flour and baking powder; mix at medium speed until the flour is just absorbed. Scrape down the dough and shape it into a disk. Wrap the disk in plastic wrap and refrigerate for 1 hour.
3. Preheat the oven to 350°F (180°C). Line a baking sheet with parchment paper.
4. Divide the dough into 24 equal pieces. Roll each piece into a rope about 4 inches (10 cm) long and 1 inch (2.5 cm) thick. With a knife, make a few lines in the rope that mimic the lines on a finger. Leave about 1 inch (2.5 cm) of space at each end and in the middle of the rope. Gently press a whole almond onto the end of each rope and transfer them to the prepared baking sheet, spacing them about 1 inch (2.5 cm) apart. Place the baking sheet in the freezer for 10 minutes before baking.
5. Bake until the bottoms of the cookies begin to brown, about 15 minutes. Let cool for 15 minutes before handling.
6. Once cool, remove the almonds from the cookies. With your finger, brush the cavity with some strawberry jam and place the almond over the jam. You can also dip the other end of the cookie in jam, if desired.

Nonna Carmela Tornatore's

OSSA DEI MORTI

BONES OF THE DEAD COOKIES

Prep time: 8 hours 30 minutes
Cook time: 22 minutes
Yield: About 48 cookies

Nonna Carmela bakes these unique cookies whose name literally translates to "bones of the dead." They are given to children as a way to explain how the people we love pass on. The process of preparing *ossa dei morti* can be a bit tricky. The cookie dough must rest for at least 8 hours so that the outside of the dough dries out and the sugar completely separates from the flour during the baking process. The result is a cookie with two distinct colors and textures. One side is dark, hard, and crunchy, and the other is white and meringue-like.

2½ cups (300 g) all-purpose or 00 flour, plus more for dusting
1 pound (455 g) confectioners' sugar
1½ teaspoons baking powder
1 teaspoon ground cloves
Zest of 1 lemon
4 large eggs, beaten

1. Line three baking sheets with parchment paper.
2. In a large bowl, whisk together the flour, confectioners' sugar, baking powder, cloves, and lemon zest. Add the eggs and, with a spatula, stir until the dry ingredients are absorbed and everything is well combined.
3. Lightly flour a work surface and turn the dough out onto it. Flour your hands and knead by hand until a ball of dough forms, about 5 minutes (it may be sticky), then divide it into 6 pieces. Working one at a time, roll each piece into a 1-inch (2.5 cm) thick rope, cut it into 1½-inch (4 cm) pieces, and place them 2 inches (5 cm) apart on the prepared baking sheets. (The sugar from the cookies will spread out, so you want to leave enough room.) Cover the baking sheets with clean kitchen towels and let rest at room temperature for at least 8 hours or up to overnight.
4. Preheat the oven to 350°F (180°C).
5. Bake the cookies until the internal sugar of the cookie has come out and resembles white meringue, about 22 minutes. Cool before handling. The cookies will be very hard, but are perfect for dipping into coffee.

Nonna Romana Sciddurlo's

OCCHI DI SANTA LUCIA

TARALLI OF SAINT LUCY

Prep time: 3 hours or overnight
Cook time: 25 minutes
Yield: About 120 taralli

Occhi di Santa Lucia are tiny, sweet taralli from Puglia made throughout the month of December, especially to celebrate Saint Lucy's Day on December 13. They are coated with a glaze that Nonna Romana refers to as *u gilepp*, which gives them a white sugar finish as they dry. Santa Lucia is the patron saint of the blind, her name being a derivative of the word for light. She is often depicted holding a plate with eyes on it and a palm branch that symbolizes victory over evil. These taralli are made very small to resemble the eyes of Santa Lucia, using a simple dough typical of the region. (It's actually the same dough as *cartellate* on page 161!)

TARALLI

1 cup (240 ml) dry white wine, such as Pinot Grigio, at room temperature

¼ cup (60 ml) olive oil

3 cups (360 g) all-purpose or 00 flour, plus more for dusting

GLAZE

1 cup (200 g) sugar

1. **To make the taralli:** Preheat the oven to 375°F (190°C). Line a baking sheet with parchment paper.
2. In the bowl of a stand mixer fitted with the dough hook attachment, mix the wine and olive oil at low speed for 1 minute. Add the flour; mix at low speed until the flour is completely absorbed and a dough forms, about 5 minutes.
3. Lightly flour a work surface and turn the dough out onto it. Knead by hand until the dough is supple, about 5 minutes.
4. Take a small chunk of dough and roll it into a rope about ¼ inch (6 mm) thick. Cut 2-inch (5 cm) pieces of dough from the rope. Wrap the pieces around your pinky finger to form a little ring and connect the ends before transferring to the prepared baking sheet. Repeat with the remaining dough.
5. Bake until the bottoms are golden and the taralli are crunchy, 20 to 25 minutes. Let cool completely before glazing.
6. Place a large sheet of aluminum foil on a work surface and set a wire rack over it.
7. **To make the glaze:** In a medium saucepan over medium-high heat, bring ½ cup (120 ml) of water and the sugar to a boil. Boil, stirring constantly, for 5 minutes. Remove from the heat and transfer to a large metal bowl.
8. Add all the taralli to the glaze and toss with a wooden spoon to coat. Continue stirring until the sugar becomes tacky and the mixture becomes difficult to stir, 7 to 10 minutes. The sugar will still be clear. Turn the taralli out onto the wire rack. Let rest for 10 minutes. Separate the taralli so they aren't touching and let them dry until the sugar turns white, 2 to 3 hours or overnight.

Nonna Lydia Palermo's

CUCCIA

SICILIAN WHEAT BERRY AND RICOTTA PUDDING

Prep time: 10 minutes
Cook time: 45 minutes
Yield: 6 to 8 servings

Nonna Lydia tells me that according to a Palermitano legend, there was a great famine in Sicily in the mid-1600s, and the people were desperate to find food to nourish their families. On December 13, which happened to be the feast day of Saint Lucy, a ship miraculously appeared in the port containing bundles of wheat, and the people rejoiced. Not having the patience to wait for the wheat to be brought to the mills and ground into flour, they decided to quickly cook the wheat with some oil and salt, and eat it right away. Over the years, *cuccia* has evolved into a pudding of cooked wheat berries and sweetened ricotta, eaten once a year to celebrate the feast of Saint Lucy in Sicily.

1 cup (180 g) hulled wheat, rinsed
1 teaspoon salt
14 ounces (400 g) whole-milk ricotta
½ cup (100 g) sugar
¼ cup (36 g) citron, cut into ¼-inch (6 mm) dice
¼ cup (44 g) candied orange peel, cut into ¼-inch (6 mm) dice
Pinch ground cinnamon
Bittersweet chocolate, for shaving and garnishing

1 In a large saucepan, bring 4 cups (960 ml) of water, the hulled wheat, and the salt to a boil over high heat. Reduce the heat to medium and cook until the wheat is tender, 40 to 45 minutes. If you like your wheat a bit softer, continue cooking for an additional 10 minutes, or until the desired texture is reached.
2 Meanwhile, in a large bowl, stir together the ricotta, sugar, citron, orange peel, and cinnamon until well combined.
3 Drain the wheat and let cool to room temperature.
4 Add the cooled wheat to the ricotta cream and mix until fully incorporated.
5 Spoon into bowls and garnish with chocolate shavings.

Nonna Lydia Palermo's

SPAGHETTINI CON PROSCIUTTO E SPINACI

THIN SPAGHETTI WITH PROSCIUTTO, SPINACH, AND RAISINS

Prep time: 15 minutes
Cook time: 15 minutes
Yield: 4 to 6 servings

This is Nonna Lydia's go-to pasta when she needs to feed a big group in a hurry, while still keeping things effortlessly chic (just like her). The simple savory and sweet flavors seamlessly blend together and make for an elegant presentation for any celebration, Italian-style!

Salt

3 tablespoons extra-virgin olive oil

3 cloves garlic, sliced

4 ounces (113 g) prosciutto, cut into ¼-inch (6 mm) dice

16 ounces (455 g) dried thin spaghetti

½ cup (75 g) golden raisins

½ cup (68 g) pignoli (pine nuts)

5 ounces (140 g) fresh baby spinach

Grated Pecorino Romano cheese, for serving

1. Bring a medium stockpot of generously salted water to a boil over high heat.
2. In a large skillet, heat the olive oil over medium heat. Add the garlic and cook, stirring occasionally, until golden, about 1 minute. Add the prosciutto and cook, stirring frequently, for 2 to 3 minutes.
3. Drop the pasta into the boiling water and cook until al dente.
4. To the skillet, add the raisins and pignoli and cook, stirring occasionally, for 4 to 5 minutes. Add the spinach along with ½ cup (120 ml) of the pasta cooking water; cook until the spinach is just wilted. Add another ½ cup (120 ml) of the pasta cooking water. Drain the pasta and add it to the skillet; cook, tossing everything together, for 1 minute.
5. Serve in warm bowls with a generous sprinkle of grated Pecorino Romano.

Nonna Nina Labruna's

CILIEGIE CON VIN SANTO

CHERRIES IN SWEET WINE

Prep time: 5 minutes
Cook time: 10 minutes
Yield: 4 to 6 servings

When guests drop by Nonna Nina's fabulous Manhattan apartment on the Upper East Side, she likes to serve them something simple and sophisticated. This sweet cherry sauce is easy to prepare, especially if using frozen cherries, and is magical on top of gelato or some panna cotta. Vin Santo is a sweet wine from Tuscany, where Nonna Nina is from, and it is smooth and sweet when paired with the slightly sour cherries.

12 ounces (340 g) fresh or thawed frozen cherries, pitted, and halved

5 tablespoons Vin Santo, divided

3 tablespoons sugar

2½ tablespoons fresh lemon juice

1 packet (½ ounce/15 g) Italian vanilla powder or 2 teaspoons vanilla extract

Pinch salt

1½ tablespoons cornstarch

1. In a small saucepan, bring the cherries, ¼ cup (60 ml) of the Vin Santo, the sugar, lemon juice, vanilla, and salt to a boil over medium-high heat. Reduce the heat to low and cook, stirring until thickened, 5 to 7 minutes.
2. In a small bowl, whisk together the cornstarch and remaining 1 tablespoon Vin Santo; add to the saucepan and remove from the heat. Stir until the mixture coats the back of a spoon, 1 to 2 minutes.

Nonna Romana Sciddurlo's

DOLCI DELLA SPOSA

WEDDING PASTRIES

Prep time: 30 minutes
Cook time: 30 minutes
Yield: 12 pastries

If you peek into the pastry shops in Puglia, you will see many of these lovely cream cakes staring back at you. *Dolci della sposa* literally translates to "sweets of the bride." They are traditionally made to celebrate weddings and brought to a bride's house on her wedding day as friends and family gather to watch her get ready for the big event. Nonna Romana starts with little domes of Italian sponge cake that she soaks in rum and fills with smooth Pastry Cream (page 6). Traditionally, the glaze would be prepared by melting sugar and water on the stove and then working in lemon juice on a piece of glass or marble, producing a thick white glaze that dries hard. Over the years, Nonna has come to prefer a simpler glaze made with confectioners' sugar, milk, and just a little vanilla. Candied cherries are used to decorate and make an elegant presentation.

CAKES

Nonstick cooking spray, for greasing
2 cups (240 g) all-purpose or 00 flour
1½ teaspoons baking powder
5 large eggs, at room temperature
1 cup (200 g) granulated sugar
3 tablespoons white rum
1 Pastry Cream recipe (page 6)

GLAZE

4½ cups (540 g) confectioners' sugar
½ cup (120 ml) whole milk
1 packet (½ ounce/15 g) Italian vanilla powder or 1 teaspoon clear vanilla extract

DECORATION

12 candied cherries

1. **To make the cakes:** Preheat the oven to 350°F (180°C). Coat two oven-safe 6-cavity silicone half-sphere molds with cooking spray, and place them on a baking sheet.
2. In a small bowl, whisk together the flour and baking powder.
3. In the bowl of a stand mixer fitted with the paddle attachment, beat the eggs and granulated sugar at medium speed for 30 seconds. Increase the speed to high and beat until the mixture is pale yellow, has doubled in volume, and ribbons form, 15 to 20 minutes.
4. With the mixer running at low speed, spoon in the dry ingredients, a little at a time, mixing until fully absorbed.
5. Fill each half-sphere mold with ¼ cup (60 ml) of batter. Bake until the cakes are golden and springy in the middle, about 20 minutes. Let cool to room temperature.
6. **To assemble the cakes:** In a small bowl, combine the rum and 3 tablespoons of water. Transfer the pastry cream to a disposable pastry bag or a resealable plastic bag with a lower corner snipped off.

CONTINUED ON PAGE 217

CONTINUED FROM PAGE 215

7 Using a very sharp knife, slice the domes off the tops of the cakes so they have a straight edge. Discard or eat the scraps. Slice the cakes in half horizontally, making sure the bottom piece is at least ½ inch (12 mm) thick. Brush both halves of each cake with the rum-water mixture.

8 Lay a piece of aluminum foil on a clean work surface, and place a wire rack on top. Pipe a thin layer of pastry cream on the bottom half of each cake and top with the other half of the cake. If any cream peeks out, smooth it out with a knife or a spatula so it's flush. Place on the prepared rack.

9 **To make the glaze:** In a medium bowl, whisk together the confectioners' sugar, milk, and vanilla until blended and smooth.

10 Spoon the glaze over the cakes, making sure all sides are well coated. Top each with a candied cherry. Let the glaze dry completely before placing the cakes in jumbo paper cupcake liners.

INDEX

A

B

C

F

G

H

I

L

M

Q

R

S

T

V

W

Z

ABOUT THE AUTHOR

Rossella Rago is a first-generation Italian American with deep roots in Mola di Bari, a small fishing village in Puglia, Italy. She holds a bachelor's degree in Italian literature from St. John's University, but her true culinary education began at home, learning to cook from her maternal grandmother, Romana, while they lived together in Brooklyn during her college years.

In 2009, Rossella launched the groundbreaking web series *Cooking with Nonna* on YouTube, becoming the first social media influencer to cook with Italian grandmothers (*nonne*), sharing their stories and treasured family recipes. Her passion for preserving Italian culinary traditions has led her to author three cookbooks: *Cooking With Nonna* (Race Point Publishing, 2017), *Cooking With Nonna: A Year of Italian Holidays* (Race Point Publishing, 2018), and *Cooking With Nonna: Sunday Dinners with La Famiglia* (Harper Celebrate, 2022).

As the founder of Bottega Della Nonna, an online retail platform specializing in Italian American novelty products and Italian imports, Rossella continues to celebrate her heritage. She is also a cohost of the *Italian American Podcast.* Beyond her digital presence, Rossella guides bespoke culinary tours in Italy, offering travelers an immersive experience in the rich food traditions of her ancestral homeland.

I dedicate this book to my beloved Nonna Romana, who thinks Tupperware is a complete waste of money and expiration dates mean nothing. The whole world wishes you were their nonna and I am so lucky you're mine.

This edition published in 2026 by Rock Point,
an imprint of The Quarto Group,
135 West 36th Street, 13th Floor,
New York, NY 10018, USA
(212) 779-4972
www.Quarto.com

First published in 2018 as *Cooking with Nonna: A Year of Italian Holidays*
by Race Point Publishing, an imprint of The Quarto Group,
135 West 36th Street, 13th Floor, New York, NY 10018, USA.

EEA Representation, WTS Tax d.o.o.,
Žanova ulica 3, 4000 Kranj, Slovenia.
www.wts-tax.si

Rock Point titles are also available at discount for retail, wholesale, promotional, and bulk purchase. For details, contact the Special Sales Manager by email at specialsales@quarto.com or by mail at The Quarto Group, Attn: Special Sales Manager, 100 Cummings Center, Suite 265D Beverly, MA 01915 USA.

10 9 8 7 6 5 4 3 2 1

ISBN: 978-1-57715-572-0

Digital edition published in 2026
eISBN: 978-1-57715-636-9

Library of Congress Control Number: 2025944756

Publisher: Rage Kindelsperger
Editorial Director: Erin Canning
Creative Director: Laura Drew
Managing Editor: Cara Donaldson
Editor: Kristy Mucci
Cover and Interior Design: Casey Schuurman
Photographer: Colin Cooke
Food Stylist: Michaela Hayes

Printed in Huizhou City, Guangdong, China TT122025